the end of me/

D1218558

Copyright © 2019 City on a Hill Studio, LLC

All rights reserved. No portion of this book may be reproduced, stored in a retrieval system, or transmitted in any form or by any means – electronic, mechanical, photocopy, recording, scanning, or other – except for brief quotations in critical reviews or articles, without prior written permission of the publisher.

Published in Louisville, Kentucky by City on a Hill Studio. City on a Hill Studio is a registered trademark of City on a Hill Studio, LLC.

Editing by Rachel Popham
Design by Nicole Enders

Scripture quotations are taken from the HOLY BIBLE: New International Version® Copyright © 1973, 1978, 1984, 2011 by Biblica, Inc. Used by permission. All rights reserved.

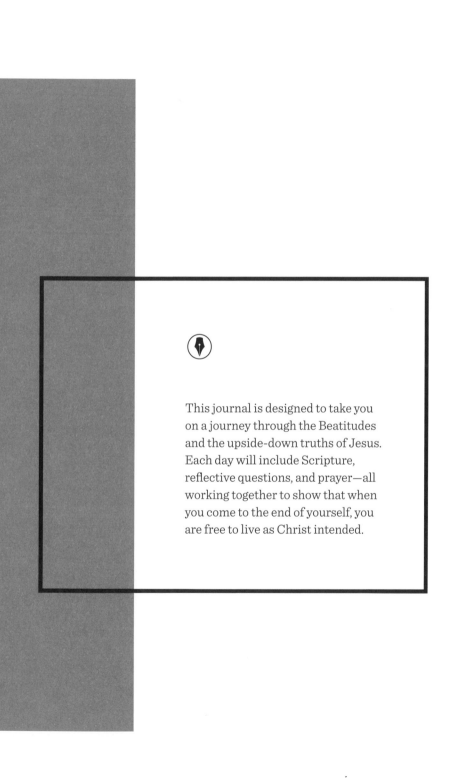

This journal is designed to take you on a journey through the Beatitudes and the upside-down truths of Jesus. Each day will include Scripture, reflective questions, and prayer—all working together to show that when you come to the end of yourself, you are free to live as Christ intended.

TABLE OF

CONTENTS

INTRODUCTION

"YOU MUST BE BROKEN TO BE WHOLE, YOU MUST MOURN TO BE HAPPY, YOU MUST BE AUTHENTIC TO BE ACCEPTED, AND YOU MUST BE EMPTY TO BE FILLED."

N early two thousand years ago, Jesus led his followers up a small mountain in the region of Galilee and sat down. As crowds of interested people gathered in and sat around him, he began to teach. His topic? The truly "Good Life."

Revolutionaries often escaped with their followers to the mountains, but this was different. Jesus was a revolutionary, and he was teaching an alternate way of life. But it wasn't quite what anyone expected. The Good Life, he insisted, was not found in revolution, in conquest, or in new-found authority, but quite the opposite.

In Jesus's famous Sermon on the Mount, found in Matthew 5 through 7, the Good Life is not one full of comfort, stability, acceptance, and status. Counterintuitively, Jesus says, it is blessed to be poor. Blessed to mourn. Blessed to be hungry and thirsty. Blessed to be pure and merciful. Blessed even to be rejected and persecuted.

Jesus opens his sermon—a sort of new law for the new people of God—with a series of blessings, called beatitudes. In the Beatitudes, everything is upside down. Brokenness is the way to wholeness. Mourning is the way to happiness. Authenticity is the way to acceptance. And emptiness is the way to fullness.

But the further we look into Jesus's words, we discover he wasn't actually turning the world upside down. He was turning our world right-side up.

Jesus's Beatitudes demonstrate a life of true blessedness—the truly Good Life.

True blessedness isn't found by in looking within ourselves or developing self-esteem. It isn't found by focusing on ourselves at all. Instead, blessedness is found in less of me and more of Christ.

The Good Life comes only at the end of me.

In this four-week study journal, return to that first-century hillside with Jesus and the disciples. Sit among the crowd and listen in on Jesus's words afresh. Receive his invitation to come to the end of yourself—and in doing so, find what you've always been searching for.

Through the Beatitudes and Kyle Idleman's book *The End of Me,* discover that:
You must be broken to be whole,
You must mourn to be happy,
You must be authentic to be accepted,
You must be empty to be filled.

When you come to the end of yourself, you are free to live as Christ intended.

HOW TO USE THIS JOURNAL

This journal is designed to take you deeper into the counterintuitive, inside-out teachings of Jesus. Each day, you'll reflect on a portion of Scripture, memorize a phrase or verse from the Beatitudes, and read a short section of *The End of Me*. Our goal is to journey together into the powerful, life-changing words of Christ.

I invite you to study and memorize Matthew 5:1-12 over the next four weeks.

NOW WHEN JESUS SAW THE CROWDS, HE WENT UP ON A MOUNTAINSIDE AND SAT DOWN. HIS DISCIPLES CAME TO HIM, AND HE BEGAN TO TEACH THEM. HE SAID:

"BLESSED ARE THE POOR IN SPIRIT,
FOR THEIRS IS THE KINGDOM OF HEAVEN.
BLESSED ARE THOSE WHO MOURN,
FOR THEY WILL BE COMFORTED.
BLESSED ARE THE MEEK,
FOR THEY WILL INHERIT THE EARTH.
BLESSED ARE THOSE WHO HUNGER AND THIRST FOR RIGHTEOUSNESS,
FOR THEY WILL BE FILLED.
BLESSED ARE THE MERCIFUL,
FOR THEY WILL BE SHOWN MERCY.
BLESSED ARE THE PURE IN HEART,
FOR THEY WILL SEE GOD.
BLESSED ARE THE PEACEMAKERS,
FOR THEY WILL BE CALLED CHILDREN OF GOD.
BLESSED ARE THOSE WHO ARE PERSECUTED BECAUSE OF RIGHTEOUSNESS,
FOR THEIRS IS THE KINGDOM OF HEAVEN.
"BLESSED ARE YOU WHEN PEOPLE INSULT YOU, PERSECUTE YOU AND FALSELY SAY ALL KINDS OF EVIL AGAINST YOU BECAUSE OF ME. REJOICE AND BE GLAD, BECAUSE GREAT IS YOUR REWARD IN HEAVEN, FOR IN THE SAME WAY THEY PERSECUTED THE PROPHETS WHO WERE BEFORE YOU.

- MATTHEW 5:1-12 (NIV)

My hope and prayer for you is that this journal serves as a guide on your journey into the truly blessed life.

Consider making this more than just another book or another task to complete. Consider committing to a 28-day journey into life in Christ! This study journal has 28 days, including four days to catch up and review. That's 28 days saturated in Jesus's words.

Imagine what God might do in your heart and mind through this four-week journey!

If you are reading *The End of Me* book by Kyle Idleman along with this journal, consider reading the corresponding chapters each week:

JOURNAL	*THE END OF ME* BOOK	THEMES	SCRIPTURE MEMORY
WEEK 1	INTRO & CHAPTER 1	BROKENNESS & WHOLENESS	MATT. 5:1-3
WEEK 2	CHAPTERS 2, 3	MOURNING & HAPPINESS	MATT. 5:4-7
WEEK 3	CHAPTER 4	AUTHENTICITY & ACCEPTANCE	MATT. 5:8-10
WEEK 4	CHAPTERS 5-8	EMPTINESS & FULLNESS	MATT. 5:11-12

MEMORIZING THE BEATITUDES

I want to encourage you to memorize the Beatitudes during this four-week journey. At only eight core statements and twelve total verses, this is a manageable task that will bear enormous fruit in your life for years to come.

Imagine having Jesus's words in the back of your mind every day. How might your daily life be different with Christ's vision for wholeness and flourishing at hand? How might your view of brokenness change? How might you respond to pain and suffering differently? Where might you become more authentic? How might you discover fullness in Christ that you never expected?

If you've never memorized Scripture, it can be intimidating. However, it's not as difficult as it might seem at first. Consider the following Scripture memory tips:

- Read the memory verse or phrase aloud several times
- Take a few minutes to reflect on the meaning of the verse or phrase
- Consider how the verse or phrase connects to the rest of the memory passage
- Rehearse the entire passage aloud and add the new memory verse or phrase
- Write out the verse, phrase, or entire passage on a note card and put it somewhere visible—on your mirror, in your car, or on your computer screen
- Consider including the verse numbers if that helps you keep your place

For example, if you are memorizing verse 4, say aloud:

"*Matthew Five*: *One* Now when Jesus saw the crowds, he went up on a mountainside and sat down. His disciples came to him, *Two* and he began to teach them. He said: *Three* Blessed are the poor in spirit, for theirs is the kingdom of heaven.

Four Blessed are those who mourn, for they will be comforted.
Four Blessed are those who mourn, for they will be comforted.
Four Blessed are those who mourn, for they will be comforted."

At the end of each day, you will find questions for your reflection. These questions are split into two categories, Content and Meaning & Meditation and Application.

CONTENT AND MEANING

The goal at this point is to ask, "What does it say?" and "What does it mean?" The questions under the heading "Content and Meaning" will help you reflect on the passage along these lines.

MEDITATION AND APPLICATION

Now that you understand the passage's content and meaning, do a second reading of the same passage. Why reread the same thing? To really savor the depth of the passage and to begin to apply its message to your life, it takes deeper reflection.

The second reading is really a "second level" reading. Think of this as a level beneath the first reading. Rather than just looking at what the passage says and means, consider what it means *for you* and what it means for you *today*. So as you read the verses again, read more slowly and thoughtfully.

The goal of this second reading is meditation—deeply engaging the truths of the passage with your heart, not just your head. Biblical meditation is not like eastern meditation, where the goal is to empty your mind. Instead, biblical meditation is about removing distractions and filling your mind with the things of God. In biblical meditation, we slow down and center ourselves on the Word.

We read and reflect not merely to learn, but to experience. God invites you to get to know him personally through his Word.

In the sections marked "Meditation and Application," you're going to be asking yourself, "What does it mean for me to obey this passage today?" and "How can I love and enjoy God more as a result of these truths?"

QUESTIONS FOR REFLECTION

EXERCISE

BEFORE DIVING INTO DAY ONE, COMPLETE THIS
SHORT EXERCISE.

HOW WOULD OUR WORLD DESCRIBE "THE GOOD LIFE"?

HOW WOULD YOU DESCRIBE JESUS'S TEACHINGS TO SOMEONE
WHO DIDN'T KNOW ANYTHING ABOUT CHRISTIANITY?

WHAT IS ONE THING YOU WANT TO GET OUT OF THIS STUDY OF
JESUS'S TEACHINGS ON BLESSEDNESS?

HOW DO YOU WANT TO BE DIFFERENT AT THE END OF THIS STUDY?

BROKEN TO BE WHOLE

Blessed are the poor in spirit, for theirs is the kingdom of heaven.

Matthew 5:3

ONE

the end of me

How would you describe the "Good Life"? If you're completely honest, and no one would know your answers, how would you respond?

The Good Life is_____.

How would you fill in the blank?
• Having a fun, easy marriage and healthy, worry-free children

•Enjoying a bottomless savings account, so I never think about expenses

•Always being surrounded by good friends and great food

•Living in a large house with a well-manicured lawn on a property with acres of freedom

•Losing fifteen pounds and being crazy good-looking

•Becoming the senior leader of my company/organization, with hundreds of people following me

•Being widely respected and even famous in my small slice of the world

Now, how do you think Jesus would answer that question?

Would he answer it generally the same way, except with a few extra provisions for holiness and giving to his Church?

It's an important question: Did Jesus come to earth, die on the cross, and rise from the grave in order to create more comfort, stability, acceptance, and status in your life?

TRULY BLESSED

In the Sermon on the Mount—Jesus's famous teaching recorded in Matthew 5 through 7—Christ reframes the Good Life. He doesn't say that there is no Good Life or that it's wrong to pursue the Good Life. Instead, he boldly announces blessings, or "beatitudes," on several groups of people. So we have a clear picture of the Good Life, direct from the Savior's heart. Here's what it means to be blessed:

> **BLESSED ARE YOU WHO ARE POOR IN SPIRIT.**
> **BLESSED ARE YOU WHO MOURN.**
> **BLESSED ARE YOU WHO ARE HUNGRY AND THIRSTY.**
> **BLESSED ARE YOU WHO ARE PURE AND MERCIFUL.**
> **BLESSED ARE YOU WHO ARE REJECTED AND PERSECUTED.**

Wait. What?

In the Beatitudes, everything is upside down. Or more accurately, Jesus is turning our world right-side up.

Jesus's Beatitudes demonstrate a life of true blessedness—the truly Good Life. True blessedness isn't found by looking within ourselves or developing self-esteem. The Good Life isn't found by focusing on me at all. Instead, blessedness is found in less of me and more of Christ.

As Kyle Idleman writes in *The End of Me*,
"These specific beatitudes will lead us, sometimes kicking and screaming, down this path to real life... Jesus will show us that blessings begin and fulfillment is found in the least likely place—the end of ourselves...Real life is found at the end of me." (page 15)

WHO IS BLESSED?

Consider, broadly, the groups of people who get Jesus's blessings: *the poor in spirit, the sorrowful, the hungry, the pure-hearted, the merciful, and the persecuted.*

What do all these people have in common? They are at the end of themselves and have nothing to offer.

Jesus starts with blessings for the "poor in spirit." Why? Poverty is to be in need, to lack resources and possessions. When talking about being poor, we might say we are broke. It's a lighthearted term, but it highlights a connection between poverty and brokenness. We think of poor people as broken people.

According to Jesus, *blessed are the broke*—the poor and broken. They are the blessed ones.

"Blessed are you when you're so broke you have nothing to offer... Jesus is saying that God's kingdom begins in you when you come to the end of yourself and realize you have nothing to offer. It's precisely the opposite of every assumption we tend to make in this world." (Idleman 28)

*Throughout this journal, you will find the page number referenced in parenthesis when a quote is taken from *The End of Me* book by Kyle Idleman.

SCRIPTURE MEMORY

66 NOW WHEN JESUS SAW THE CROWDS, HE WENT UP ON A MOUNTAINSIDE AND SAT DOWN."

- MATTHEW 5:1

This flies in the face of everything we are taught in life. Do any of these sound familiar?

The world says, "Stand up straight. Defend yourself. Get what's yours."
The way of Jesus says, "Don't think too highly of yourself (Romans 12:3). Give away what you've earned (Matthew 22:21). Take a break every now and then (Mark 2:27; Luke 10:38)."

The world says, "Pull yourself up. Get it together. Prove you have what it takes."
The way of Jesus says, "Turn the other cheek (Matthew 5:39). Don't make yourself look more spiritual than you are (Matthew 6:1). Ask for help (James 1:5)."

The world says, "Don't ask for help. Don't give in to the pain. Don't ever give up."
The way of Jesus says, "Put others first (Romans 12:10). Acknowledge your limitations (Psalm 16). Give up—and find the truly Good Life (Matthew 10:39)."

Jesus flips the script. His laws and ways cut through the world's ideas about performance and self-sufficiency.

Blessed are the poor, the broken, the needy. And if you are poor, broken, and needy?

Congratulations! You have discovered the truly Good Life.

See the section "Memorizing the Beatitudes" in the Introduction for a vision and strategy for memorizing this passage.

(TO UNDERSTAND HOW TO ANSWER THESE TWO TYPES OF QUESTIONS, SEE THE INTRODUCTION SECTION "QUESTIONS FOR REFLECTION.")

CONTENT AND MEANING

WHAT CENTRAL THEMES RUN THROUGH ALL OF THE BEATITUDES?

HOW CAN IT BE THAT HAVING NOTHING TO OFFER IS ONE OF THE CONDITIONS OF BEING CALLED BLESSED BY JESUS?

WHY IS IT IMPORTANT TO UNDERSTAND OUR NEEDS—FOR FOOD, WATER, SHELTER, RELATIONSHIPS, AND MEANING—AS HUMANS?

QUESTIONS FOR REFLECTION

MEDITATION AND APPLICATION

READ MATTHEW 5:1-3 AGAIN SLOWLY AND ANSWER THE FOLLOWING QUESTIONS.

DOES ANY PART OF YOU RESIST WHEN YOU READ KYLE'S WORDS: "REAL LIFE IS FOUND AT THE END OF ME"?

WHAT IS ONE AREA OF YOUR LIFE WHERE "ME" IS STILL RUNNING THE SHOW AND CALLING THE SHOTS?

HOW DO YOU RESONATE WITH THE PHRASES OUR WORLD PROMOTES—"GET IT TOGETHER; DON'T ASK FOR HELP"? WHERE HAVE YOU HEARD THESE WORDS IN YOUR LIFE?

HOW IS YOUR HEART MOVED BY CONSIDERING JESUS'S COUNTERINTUITIVE BLESSINGS FOR THE POOR AND NEEDY?

where blessings begin

What is the first thing that comes to your mind when you hear the word *blessing*?

Personally, I tend to equate *blessing* with financial and material abundance. I think of receiving a surprise check in the mail just before a bill is due. I think of someone who feels slightly self-conscious about the size and cost of their house offering the statement, "It's such a blessing." And I think of smooth-selling televangelists offering *blessings* in return for a donation to their private jet fund.

But *blessing* is a much more profound, fuller word. In its original meaning lies a far greater abundance than financial or material. A better blessing exists!

BLESSEDNESS AND FLOURISHING

First, let's consider what it meant to be blessed in Jesus's world.

Jesus was speaking to one audience but in two contexts. The Jewish listeners on that grassy

> "YOU FLOURISH WHEN YOU ARE POOR IN SPIRIT, WHEN YOU MOURN AND WHEN YOU ARE HUMBLED."

hillside lived between two worlds—their older Hebrew tradition, which included the songs of the Psalms and the wisdom of the Proverbs, and the newer Greco-Roman culture, which emphasized the virtues of goodness without religious tradition. But both the Hebrew tradition and the Greco-Roman culture held a similar concept at the pinnacle of their thought: human flourishing. One New Testament scholar translates these verses as "flourishing" instead of "blessed":

> **FLOURISHING ARE THE POOR IN SPIRIT BECAUSE THE KINGDOM OF HEAVEN IS THEIRS. FLOURISHING ARE THE MOURNERS BECAUSE THEY WILL BE COMFORTED. FLOURISHING ARE THE HUMBLE BECAUSE THEY WILL INHERIT THE WORLD.**

Jesus was brilliantly speaking two languages and engaging two cultures at once with his Beatitudes. The blessings would have reminded the listeners of the many promises of blessing in the Old Testament, but also of the virtues taught by Greek philosophers. In this way, Jesus was appealing to both worlds, and showing that his new "laws" fulfilled the longings of both Jewish and Gentile thought.

How does this change the way you think about Jesus's words?

Think about it like this: "You flourish when you are poor in spirit, when you mourn, and when you are humbled."

His teaching engaged both Hebrew and Greek thought but flipped both upside down, or, more appropriately, right-side up. All worldly systems begin on the premise of flourishing through achievement, comfort, and status. But our world is broken. *Jesus wants to flip us right-side up: You flourish you when you are poor in spirit.*

THE HEART OF THE SCRIPTURES

In this sense, Jesus's words in the Beatitudes, at the start of his Sermon on the Mount, get right to the core of what the Bible says about a blessed life.

"The Sermon is Christianity's answer to the greatest question that humanity has always faced—How can we experience true human flourishing? What is happiness, blessedness, shalom, and how does one obtain and sustain it? The Sermon is not the only place in the New Testament or the whole Bible that addresses this fundamental question. I would suggest that this question is at the core of the entire message of Scripture. But the Sermon is at the epicenter and, simultaneously, the forefront of the Holy Scripture's answer." (Pennington 14)

These are deep waters, so let's simplify the idea.

All of us have a deep longing to thrive, to find meaning, and to become whole. But counterintuitively, we don't thrive by *trying* to thrive, and we don't become whole by *working* toward it directly. Jesus is saying, you begin to thrive when you give up trying. You find wholeness by accepting brokenness.

Why? Because wholeness is found only in God's presence. Flourishing comes only through faith in God, oneness with Christ, and the empowerment of the Holy Spirit.

This is life in the right-side-up Kingdom: You find your life by giving it away. You gain your soul by letting go of self. You receive life—life to the full—by the death of another.

This message is at the heart of the Beatitudes, the Sermon on the Mount, and all of Scripture: *Blessed are the poor in spirit, for theirs is the Kingdom of heaven.*

Or to put it another way: Blessed are you when you come to the end of yourself.

SCRIPTURE MEMORY

" NOW WHEN JESUS SAW THE CROWDS, HE WENT UP ON A MOUNTAINSIDE AND SAT DOWN."

- MATTHEW 5:1

THE SERMON IS CHRISTIANITY'S ANSWER TO THE GREAT-EST QUESTION THAT HUMANITY HAS ALWAYS FACED—HOW CAN WE EXPERIENCE TRUE HUMAN FLOURISHING? WHAT IS HAPPINESS, BLESSEDNESS, SHALOM, AND HOW DOES ONE OBTAIN AND SUSTAIN IT? THE SERMON IS NOT THE ONLY PLACE IN THE NEW TESTAMENT OR THE WHOLE BIBLE THAT ADDRESSES THIS FUNDAMENTAL QUESTION. **I WOULD SUGGEST THAT THIS QUESTION IS AT THE CORE OF THE ENTIRE MESSAGE OF SCRIPTURE. BUT THE SERMON IS AT THE EPICENTER AND, SIMULTANEOUSLY, THE FOREFRONT OF THE HOLY SCRIPTURE'S ANSWER.**

- JONATHAN PENNINGTON

CONTENT AND MEANING

IN WHAT WAYS IS OUR CULTURE SIMILAR TO JESUS'S CULTURE? HOW IS IT DIFFERENT?

HOW DOES THE CONTEXT OF JESUS'S WORDS—SPOKEN WITHIN BOTH JEWISH AND GREEK INFLUENCE—CHANGE THE WAY YOU THINK ABOUT THEM?

HOW CAN ONE BE BOTH "POOR IN SPIRIT" IN ONE SENSE AND YET FLOURISHING?

QUESTIONS FOR REFLECTION

MEDITATION AND APPLICATION

READ MATTHEW 5:1-3 AGAIN SLOWLY AND ANSWER THE FOLLOWING QUESTIONS.

HOW WOULD YOU DESCRIBE "FLOURISHING" OR "THRIVING" IN YOUR OWN WORDS? HOW DOES YOUR DESCRIPTION DIFFER FROM JESUS'S WORDS?

WHAT FORMS OF ACHIEVEMENT, COMFORT, SECURITY, OR STATUS WOULD BE THE MOST DIFFICULT TO LAY IN THE GRAVE?

HOW DO YOU SENSE CHRIST INVITING YOU TO A DEEPER, BETTER WAY OF LIFE?

meet the poor in spirit

n America, we assume money can buy happiness. The average person would agree with the statement: "The more money I have, the happier I will be." Wouldn't you? Recently, researchers from the fields of psychology and sociology tested the hypothesis that money leads to happiness. A survey of almost two million people from more than 160 countries showed that money does lead to happiness—but only to a certain point. When our basic needs are met, and we don't have to worry about where our next meal is coming from, our emotional well-being increases. As a result, happiness and well-being peak at an income of $60,000 to $75,000 a year.

However, after that point, and especially above an annual income of $95,000, additional money *decreases* happiness. The lead researchers believe that wealth beyond basic comfort and daily needs begin to decrease our well-being rapidly.

In other words, money can't buy happiness—it might even prevent happiness.

THE POOR IN SPIRIT

We have seen that Jesus's words in the Beatitudes shake up conventional wisdom. Broken is whole. Empty is full. Poor is rich.

But what exactly does it mean to be "poor in spirit"? And why are the poor in spirit *blessed*?

Yesterday, we described Jesus's use of "blessed" as a state of wholeness through human flourishing. And we have seen that we often equate poverty with brokenness—we casually say "I'm broke." So how can it be that poverty and brokenness are the paths to flourishing?

> **"Jesus says the kingdom begins with taking inventory and coming up with zero. We have nothing to offer, and that means we're making progress."**
>
> KYLE IDLEMAN

There's something the poor have that the rich lack: The poor are in *need*. They need help. They need others. They need God.

When we are in need, we discover that the accumulation of money and possessions is not the path to flourishing. Instead, money and possessions can make us feel entitled to more and more of this world. We can look down on those who have less than us. We slowly fall asleep to the reality that we are creatures of *need*.

The poor in spirit have nothing to prove. They are comfortable with being in need. They identify with the materially poor, with those who mourn, with the hungry and thirsty, and with the persecuted.

To be poor in spirit is not about having a small bank account or few possessions—although less may be more. Being poor in spirit is primarily a posture of humility.

To discover the epitome of poor in spirit, we can look to the preacher of these words. How was Jesus poor in spirit?

THE EXAMPLE OF JESUS

Jesus's life on earth illustrates what it means to be poor in spirit.

Jesus was born into ordinary circumstances and was raised without much financially. In other words, ordinary life and meager possessions are not hindrances to life with God.

Jesus was intimately committed to his family and friends—he cared for his mother and spent almost every waking minute of his public ministry leading his disciples. In other words, to be poor in spirit is to create space for others' needs and interests.

Jesus had eyes to see the value of the poor, the sick, the outcast, the brokenhearted, and the dying. In other words, poverty of spirit views itself as at the bottom of life, not the top.

Jesus challenged the religious leaders of his day, but praised those who served God without pretense or show. In other words, genuine faith and love are at the heart of the poor in spirit.

Jesus gave his own life to save the lives of many. In other words, the poor in spirit are quick to give, ready to sacrifice, and put the needs of others above their own.

THROUGH HIS POVERTY

Of course, Jesus wasn't *just* an example. His life of spiritual poverty made a way for us to have eternal life.

The apostle Paul puts it like this:

> "FOR YOU KNOW THE GRACE OF OUR LORD JESUS CHRIST, THAT THOUGH HE WAS RICH, YET FOR YOUR SAKE, HE BECAME POOR SO THAT YOU THROUGH HIS POVERTY MIGHT BECOME RICH."

> - 2 CORINTHIANS 8:9

Jesus, as the Son of God and co-Creator of the cosmos, is eternally rich. He calls the stars by name and owns the cattle on a thousand hills. The seas are calmed at his word and the dead are raised by his tears. Everything that exists is his.

And yet, in his infinite wealth, he took on poverty. He became poor in spirit so that we might become rich. The riches that he offers aren't temporary pleasures like money and possessions. No, those come and go—and don't provide true happiness anyway.

Through his poverty, Jesus gives us the most valuable thing possible: He makes us sons and daughters of God. He lived the perfect life that we have resisted. He died the brutal death that our own sins demanded. And yet he was raised from the grave in victory over Satan, sin, and death.

As the first half of Romans 8:17 says,

> NOW IF WE ARE CHILDREN [OF GOD], THEN WE ARE HEIRS— HEIRS OF GOD AND CO-HEIRS WITH CHRIST.

All that is his becomes ours. Eternal riches and glory belong to us who belong to him!

But as the second half of Romans 8:17 says,

> WE ARE HEIRS—HEIRS OF GOD AND CO-HEIRS WITH CHRIST—IF INDEED WE SHARE IN HIS SUFFERINGS IN ORDER THAT WE MAY ALSO SHARE IN HIS GLORY.

In Christ, we have an eternal inheritance. And in Christ, we can participate in his life here and now, but it will mean suffering. Did you catch that?

Oneness with Christ in his riches requires oneness with Christ in his poverty. And yet, even in the call to suffer, there's a path to glory—"that we may also share in his glory."

This is life in the upside-down kingdom: Poverty on earth means riches for all eternity. If we want to be like Christ in his glory, then we must become like Christ in his poverty of spirit.

As Jesus himself said, "It is more blessed to give than to receive." (Acts 20:35)

SCRIPTURE MEMORY

> " NOW WHEN JESUS SAW THE CROWDS, HE WENT UP ON A MOUNTAINSIDE AND SAT DOWN. AND HE BEGAN TO TEACH THEM. HE SAID: "
>
> - MATTHEW 5:1-2

CONTENT AND MEANING

WHAT DOES IT MEAN TO BE "POOR IN SPIRIT" IN YOUR OWN WORDS?

WHY DO YOU THINK JESUS'S VERY FIRST BEATITUDE IS A BLESSING ON THE POOR IN SPIRIT? HOW DOES THIS PROVIDE A GATEWAY INTO THE OTHER BEATITUDES?

IN WHAT WAYS DID JESUS DEMONSTRATE POVERTY OF SPIRIT IN HIS EARTHLY LIFE?

HOW DOES JESUS'S BECOMING POOR LEAD TO OUR RICHES (2 CORINTHIANS 8:9)? HOW DOES THIS CHANGE THE WAY YOU THINK OF SALVATION AND ETERNAL LIFE?

MEDITATION AND APPLICATION

READ MATTHEW 5:1-3 AGAIN SLOWLY AND ANSWER THE FOLLOWING QUESTIONS.

IF JESUS HAD BEEN BORN INTO A WEALTHY FAMILY, NEVER EXPERIENCED NEED, AND LIVED A LAVISH LIFESTYLE, WOULD THAT CHANGE HOW YOU VIEWED HIM?

WHEN KYLE WRITES, "WHEN WE HAVE NOTHING TO OFFER, WE ARE MAKING PROGRESS," HOW DO YOU RESPOND TO THIS STATEMENT?

WHO COMES TO MIND WHEN YOU THINK OF POVERTY OF SPIRIT? WHAT CHRISTIANS DO YOU KNOW THAT FIT THIS DESCRIPTION, AND WHAT IS IT ABOUT THEM THAT YOU ADMIRE?

beautifully broken

n *The End of Me* video series, Kyle Idleman highlights the testimony of Rachelle Starr to demonstrate the power of brokenness and wholeness. Rachelle grew up in a stable, Christian home, but drifted from the Lord in early adulthood. Despite a healthy marriage and a thriving career, Rachelle felt something was missing. "It was never enough," she shares in the first video of *The End of Me* video series. "This is not why I exist," she remembers thinking.

When God began to work in the hearts of Rachelle and her husband, he did so in unique and unexpected ways. One day, she was struck by the impression that God was calling her to minister his love to women in the sex industry. In a moment, Rachelle was given her calling: To serve females in the sex industry and offer them the hope of Jesus Christ.

FINDING JESUS IN A STRIP CLUB

After about a year and a half of prayer, fasting, research, and conversation, Rachelle was searching to find a name for her new ministry. After reading of Esther's scarlet colored rope on her robe in the Old Testament, she thought about that word *scarlet*.

But then she also felt the Lord telling her to get to work—this week, today, right now!

Sometime later, Rachelle found herself in a strip club with a young woman who was looking for work in order to feed her five children. She had been drinking all day to mute the shame of taking her clothes off for strangers. After getting some food, she immediately vomited all over Rachelle.

Now, this is probably not what Rachelle envisioned for herself growing up and studying through school.

We think what will satisfy us is pursuing our own desires, wants, needs—finding happiness for ourselves. Why wouldn't we? But remember: Jesus takes everything we thought we knew, and he turns it upside down.

The first beatitude is about reaching the end of yourself—"Blessed are the poor in spirit, for theirs is the kingdom of heaven." To be poor in spirit is to be at the end of ourselves, to have nothing left to offer. And Jesus says, that's where God's blessing will meet you.

There's a blessing for the broken.

Rachelle continued to serve and love this woman, despite the vomit, embarrassment, and club owner's rebuke. As Rachelle shared the love of Christ with her, this woman gave her life to Jesus and fell to her knees in prayer. After praying, the woman exclaimed in joy, "I just met Jesus here!"

As the woman began to leave the strip club with the outrageous love of God now in her heart, Rachelle asked for her name. The woman replied, "My name is Scarlet."

THE GOSPEL AND THE PROSTITUTE

In Luke 7:36-50, we read of Jesus's encounters with two very different people.

The first character is a Pharisee named Simon. He has invited Jesus and many other friends over to his house for a theological discussion. He's interested in Jesus's teachings but isn't sure if he truly believes that Jesus is who he says he is. So he shares his food and table with Jesus, but otherwise doesn't show much hospitality.

While this group of well-educated, respectable men is eating together, a woman off the streets, a biblical euphemism for a prostitute, comes in. She is our second character.

The text says:

> AS SHE STOOD AT [JESUS'S] FEET WEEPING, SHE
> BEGAN TO WET HIS FEET WITH HER TEARS. THEN
> SHE WIPED THEM WITH HER HAIR, KISSED THEM, AND
> POURED PERFUME ON THEM.

- LUKE 7:38

Now, this is an awkward situation. It would have been awkward for almost everyone in the room.

But it wasn't awkward for Jesus. He looked past this woman's history of poor decisions, grave mistakes, and outright sin. He looked into her heart and saw her need. She believed in Jesus, needed Jesus, and poured out her life for him.

Sensing the religious leaders' disdain, Jesus began to tell a story.

> SIMON, I HAVE SOMETHING TO TELL YOU...
> TWO PEOPLE OWED MONEY TO A CERTAIN
> MONEYLENDER. ONE OWED HIM FIVE
> HUNDRED DENARII, AND THE OTHER FIFTY.
> NEITHER OF THEM HAD THE MONEY TO PAY
> HIM BACK, SO HE FORGAVE THE DEBTS OF
> BOTH. NOW WHICH OF THEM WILL LOVE HIM
> MORE?
>
> - LUKE 7:40-42

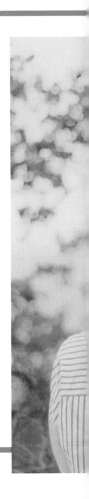

The answer is clear, and Simon gets the answer right: "The one who had the bigger debt forgiven" (v43). Jesus then describes the meaning of the parable: Simon did not greet Jesus with a kiss, and this woman couldn't stop kissing his feet. Simon didn't offer Jesus fresh water to wash up, yet this woman provided her very own tears. Simon didn't offer a drop of perfume to freshen up, but this woman poured out her most treasured possession in a kind of anointing ceremony.

The point? Jesus announces, "Her many sins have been forgiven—as her great love has shown. But whoever has been forgiven little loves little" (v47).

THE LOVE OF THE FORGIVEN

Jesus's gentle, healing love for the sinful woman overwhelmed her. She knew she was a sinner—it was plain for everyone to see. And she represents the opposite side of Jesus's statement: Whoever has been forgiven much, loves much.

Anyone who has experienced the forgiveness of Christ has been forgiven of their entire lifetime of sins. Yet, for someone who thinks their sins are small—or for someone who doesn't think they even need forgiveness, like Simon—their love for Jesus will be small.

But for one who knows they have been forgiven of much, they will love much.

This woman had nothing to offer and everything to receive. She was one who was truly poor in spirit. She was at the end of herself and was willing to lay herself down. In the presence of Jesus, she experienced true love and forgiveness.

The one who is forgiven of much loves much.
The one who is completely broken will be beautifully healed.

SCRIPTURE MEMORY

NOW WHEN JESUS SAW THE CROWDS, HE WENT
UP ON A MOUNTAINSIDE AND SAT DOWN. AND HE
BEGAN TO TEACH THEM. HE SAID: "

- MATTHEW 5:1-2

CONTENT AND MEANING

READ LUKE 7:36-50 AND CONSIDER THESE TWO CHARACTERS: SIMON AND THE SINFUL WOMAN.

HOW DO THESE TWO INDIVIDUALS REPRESENT TWO DIFFERENT WAYS OF LIVING APART FROM GOD?

WHAT IS THE CONNECTION BETWEEN FORGIVENESS AND LOVE? HOW HAVE YOU WITNESSED THIS CONNECTION IN EVERYDAY LIFE?

QUESTIONS FOR REFLECTION

MEDITATION AND APPLICATION

READ MATTHEW 5:3 AGAIN SLOWLY AND ANSWER THE FOLLOWING QUESTIONS.

HOW DO YOU SEE YOUR OWN NEED TO BECOME POOR IN SPIRIT?

IN WHAT WAYS DO YOU RELATE TO RACHELLE'S STORY—SEARCHING FOR MEANING BUT STRUGGLING TO FIND FULFILLMENT?

HOW MIGHT YOU RELATE TO SCARLET'S SITUATION—IN UTTER NEED OF A SOLUTION, BUT ENTIRELY AT THE END OF HERSELF?

the path to wholeness

n the introduction to *The End of Me*, Kyle Idleman encourages us to finish this sentence:

"Jesus became real when_____."

How would you finish the statement? When did Jesus become real to you?

BROKEN TO BECOME WHOLE

If you're like me, and like the responses that Kyle shared in his book, Jesus became real when you reached the end of yourself. For me, it was the death of my brother in a car accident when I was 16. I was absolutely crushed. And then again in my late twenties, when I was overwhelmed with depression and chronic pain; I could barely see a way through the struggle.

When was it for you? Perhaps a real tragedy brought your life crashing down. Maybe it was a relationship that broke and felt like a death. Or it may have been your sin that brought you to the end of yourself.

Whatever it was, you probably discovered that "real life is found at the end of me". (15) In an indirect sense, our greatest pains, trials, and losses can become gifts from the Lord. We wouldn't choose the pain, and we don't wish for suffering, but through the brokenness, we can become whole.

When Jesus says, "Blessed are the poor in spirit, for theirs is the kingdom of heaven," he reveals a path to us.

As Kyle writes, "These specific beatitudes will help lead us, sometimes kicking and screaming, down this path to real life... Jesus will show us that blessings begin and fulfillment is found in the least likely place—the end of ourselves." (15)

HER STORY IS OUR STORY

Think back to yesterday's study in Luke 7:36-50. The woman off the street was broken, yes. But she was *beautifully broken*. She brought her need to Jesus; she poured out her life in praise of him.

This woman had come to the end of herself. But when she looked into Jesus's eyes, she discovered that her brokenness could become wholeness. As tears filled her eyes, the other individuals in the room faded into the background. She could only see Jesus.

"The funny thing about tears," Kyle writes about this moment, "is that when they fill our eyes, that's when we can see most clearly" (31).

Jesus gives the religious leader a rebuke. But he gives the street woman a blessing: "Your sins are forgiven" (Luke 7:48).

Even if you have never sinned so publicly or felt as shamed as this woman, you can find your own story in hers. For a time, you ran from Jesus. You looked for love in all the wrong places. You found acceptance in those who could later abandon you. You spent a lifetime working toward a goal, only to find it wasn't the right goal at all.

Her story is our story. And to us and anyone who is willing to be broken, Jesus's words are:

> "YOUR FAITH HAS SAVED YOU; GO IN PEACE"
>
> - LUKE 7:50

WHO DO YOU WANT TO BE?

This passage leads us to an important question: When you read this story of Jesus, Simon, and the prostitute, in whom do you see yourself?

Many of us would prefer to be like Simon—at the top of our field, at the table of honor, hosting impressive guests with lavish catering budgets. But maybe you identify more with the woman—embarrassed and ashamed but completely in love with Christ. Or perhaps you even view yourself as Jesus in the story—assessing the hearts of others, able to judge with righteousness and offer forgiveness. (Don't get too carried away. You're not Jesus in this encounter.)

Kyle notes that this is a trick question. "Most of us want [to be] both... We want to be made whole without having to be broken" (33).

We want the power and luxury of Simon with the faith and humility of the woman. But this is not likely to work. We must be fully broken before we can be fully healed.

BROKENNESS TO WHOLENESS

Brokenness is not just a moment in life. Although it can be most fully realized in a moment of tragedy or shame, brokenness is a path. It's the path to wholeness.

Psychologist Chuck DeGroat has written that the great need of people today is to become whole in all the areas of our lives.

SCRIPTURE MEMORY

Rather than being fragmented, divided people, we must become wholehearted in our faith and life. The path to wholeness is brokenness. He writes,

"We learn wholeness when our boundaries are shattered, when our disciplines fail us, when our theologies stump us, when our supposedly wise choices betray us. We learn by un-learning, by stumbling and falling into the very thing we attempted to gain on our own terms... Like love, wholeness is discovered in a thousand disappointments, embarrassments, and missteps."

When we come to the end of ourselves and we realize that we are completely broken apart from Christ, then his great work of transformation in us can begin.

In a world trying to be strong and rich, Jesus invites us to the freedom of being poor in spirit and broken—and being made whole.

NOW WHEN JESUS SAW THE CROWDS, HE WENT UP ON A MOUNTAINSIDE AND SAT DOWN. AND HE BEGAN TO TEACH THEM. HE SAID: BLESSED ARE THE POOR IN SPIRIT, FOR THEIRS IS THE KINGDOM OF HEAVEN."

- MATTHEW 5:1-3

CONTENT AND MEANING

READ LUKE 7:36-50 AGAIN. DOES ANYTHING NEW STAND OUT TO YOU FROM YOUR SECOND READING?

HOW WOULD YOU EXPLAIN WHAT IT MEANS TO BE BROKEN? WHAT ABOUT TO BE WHOLE?

WHAT IS THE CONNECTION BETWEEN BEING POOR IN SPIRIT AND BEING BROKEN?

MEDITATION AND APPLICATION

READ MATTHEW 5:1-3 AGAIN SLOWLY AND ANSWER THE FOLLOWING QUESTIONS.

HOW DID YOU FEEL AS YOU REFLECTED ON THE OPENING STATEMENT ("JESUS BECAME REAL TO ME WHEN...")? WHAT DIFFERENT EXPERIENCES OR RELATIONSHIPS CAME TO MIND?

HOW HAVE YOU EXPERIENCED LOSS LEADING TO GAIN? HOW HAVE YOU EXPERIENCED AN AWARENESS OF YOUR BROKENNESS OFFERING YOU WHOLENESS?

TO QUOTE DR. DEGROAT, HOW HAVE YOU EXPERIENCED THAT "WHOLENESS IS DISCOVERED IN A THOUSAND DISAPPOINTMENTS, EMBARRASSMENTS, AND MISSTEPS"?

theirs is the kingdom

Throughout most of Week 1, we have been exploring the first half of this famous beatitude: "Blessed are the poor in spirit..." It's a shocking way to begin! It certainly captures our attention and causes us to wonder what Jesus meant. Hopefully, you have spent the last five days discovering that brokenness is a way to wholeness.

But how does the blessing end?

"Blessed are the poor in spirit... *for theirs is the kingdom of heaven.*"

What does this mean? Why does the blessing for the poor in spirit promise the kingdom of heaven?

THEIRS IS THE KINGDOM OF HEAVEN

First of all, notice what this phrase is not. It is not a blessing that follows a command. Jesus doesn't say, "If you become poor in spirit, you will receive the kingdom of heaven." Instead, Jesus is simply announcing blessings: "Blessed are you!" He blesses before he commands and gives

help before he gives law.

It is a blessing on the already poor in spirit to be given the kingdom of heaven. So, what exactly does that mean?

The original Greek indicates that *theirs* is exclusive, meaning the poor in spirit will be given the kingdom and the *not* poor in spirit will *not* be given the kingdom. These are serious words!

There are both present and future dynamics to the promise of the kingdom of heaven. For the poor in spirit, Jesus is announcing that they *immediately* receive the kingdom, and yet some aspects of the kingdom will come in the *future* eternal life.

In fact, this is true of all promises of the kingdom of heaven. The kingdom is where God reigns and rules, where what he says goes. God is the King, and we exist in his kingdom. The kingdom, then, is living under and with God.

The kingdom of heaven (are you ready for it?) is the Good Life!

In one sense, we are already in the kingdom, since we are already with God. In another sense, we will one day be *fully* in the kingdom, where God will reign unopposed after disposing of all sin, evil, and brokenness.

The promise *today* for the poor in spirit: You are already with God! You belong to his eternal kingdom! Heaven has come to earth. You poor in spirit are blessed; yours is the kingdom of heaven!

And there's a *future* hope for the poor in spirit: One day, your poverty will be turned to abundance; you will be filled to the full! Your lowly status will be replaced with glory; your troubles will come to an end. Look forward to this great and eternal kingdom!

Surely this is two-fold good news for the poor in spirit. But how do we enter into this?

HEALED BY HIS WOUNDS

The good news for the poor in spirit is that the thing they might despise most—their poverty, their need, their lack—is the very thing that Jesus calls "blessed." We might want to hide our flaws, our mistakes, and our scars.

But in Jesus's world, the broken are the most valuable.

In a powerful prophecy given hundreds of years before Jesus's birth, the prophet Isaiah wrote of Jesus,

BUT HE WAS PIERCED FOR OUR
TRANSGRESSIONS, HE WAS CRUSHED FOR OUR
INIQUITIES; THE PUNISHMENT THAT BROUGHT
US PEACE WAS ON HIM, AND BY HIS WOUNDS
WE ARE HEALED.

- ISAIAH 53:5

As Kyle writes, the word "wounded" here refers to actual bruises caused by broken blood vessels, while the word "healed" means to be mended, repaired, or made whole. We are healed, made whole, because Jesus was bruised, wounded, and broken for us.

"And it's only after we have been made whole that we are ready to fulfill our purpose and be used by God. That's the inside-out way of Jesus—in you, then through you." (Idleman 39)

SCRIPTURE MEMORY

NOW WHEN JESUS SAW   THE CROWDS, HE
WENT UP ON A MOUNTAINSIDE AND SAT
DOWN. AND HE BEGAN TO TEACH THEM. HE
SAID: BLESSED ARE THE POOR IN SPIRIT, FOR
THEIRS IS THE KINGDOM OF HEAVEN."

- MATTHEW 5:1-3

CONTENT AND MEANING

WHO IS JESUS DESCRIBING WHEN HE REFERS TO "THE POOR IN SPIRIT"? WHAT DOES IT MEAN THAT "THEIRS IS THE KINGDOM OF HEAVEN"?

HOW WOULD YOU DEFINE AND DESCRIBE "THE KINGDOM OF HEAVEN"? HOW IS IT DIFFERENT FROM "THE KINGDOM OF EARTH" OR "THE KINGDOM OF THIS WORLD"?

WHY DO YOU THINK JESUS CHOOSES THIS PARTICULAR PROMISE FOR THE POOR IN SPIRIT—THAT "THEIRS IS THE KINGDOM OF HEAVEN"?

QUESTIONS FOR REFLECTION

MEDITATION AND APPLICATION

READ MATTHEW 5:1-3 AGAIN SLOWLY AND ANSWER THE FOLLOWING QUESTIONS.

IN WHAT WAYS DO YOU IDENTIFY WITH THE POOR IN SPIRIT? IN WHAT WAYS DO YOU STRUGGLE TO IDENTIFY AS POOR IN SPIRIT?

HOW HAS THIS STUDY IN A SINGLE VERSE CHANGED THE WAY YOU THINK ABOUT JESUS, YOURSELF, AND THE GOOD LIFE?

HOW ARE YOU CURRENTLY EXPERIENCING THE KINGDOM— LIFE WITH GOD—AND HOW DO YOU LOOK FORWARD TO EXPERIENCING THE KINGDOM IN FULLNESS IN THE FUTURE?

REFLECTION & REVIEW

O n the seventh day of each week, we're going to pause to review and reflect on the past week.

If you are behind a day or two, use this day to catch up.

If you are caught up, use this day to review the previous six days' notes—especially all the Scripture references and stories. Use these seventh days to review your Scripture memory verses as well.

SCRIPTURE MEMORY

REVIEW MATTHEW 5:1-3

NOW WHEN JESUS SAW THE CROWDS, HE WENT UP ON A MOUNTAINSIDE AND SAT DOWN. AND HE BEGAN TO TEACH THEM. HE SAID: BLESSED ARE THE POOR IN SPIRIT, FOR THEIRS IS THE KINGDOM OF HEAVEN.

QUESTIONS FOR REFLECTION

BASED ON YOUR WEEK'S READING AND REFLECTION, ANSWER THE FOLLOWING QUESTIONS.

WHAT WAS THE MOST SIGNIFICANT THING I LEARNED ABOUT JESUS AND THE CHRISTIAN LIFE THIS WEEK?

WHAT WAS THE MOST SIGNIFICANT THING I LEARNED ABOUT POVERTY OF SPIRIT, BROKENNESS, AND WHOLENESS THIS WEEK?

WHAT WAS THE MOST SIGNIFICANT THING I LEARNED ABOUT MYSELF THIS WEEK?

WHAT WOULD MY LIFE LOOK LIKE IF I FULLY BELIEVED AND LIVED EVERYTHING I READ AND WROTE THIS WEEK?

MOURN TO BE HAPPY

Blessed are those who mourn,
for they will be comforted.

Matthew 5:4

TWO

those who mourn

We all want to be happy. We want to be free, joyful, peaceful, and thriving.

It follows, then, that we do *not* want to be sad. We do not want to endure loss, to mourn, to grieve, and to be sorrowful, even depressed.

Just glance at the magazine covers at the grocery store checkout lane. What do you see? Smiling faces, laughing couples, thin bodies, exquisite meals, and glamorous homes. What do you *not* see? Unhappy people, broken relationships (unless it's juicy breakup gossip, I suppose), and ordinary-looking meals and homes.

In general, we are all pursuing our own happiness. And here's the thing: We should!

But we should know where true joy can be found and apply our lives to discovering and maintaining that joy and peace.

Spoiler alert: True happiness is not found in constant ease, airbrushed appearances, and the abundance of possessions.

THE DOWN AND OUT

Last week, we looked at Jesus's words:

> BLESSED ARE THE POOR
> IN SPIRIT, FOR THEIRS
> IS THE KINGDOM OF
> HEAVEN
> - MATTHEW 5:3

We discovered that, in Jesus's upside-down kingdom, the truly blessed ones are those who are poor, lowly, bankrupt, and broken. Those who have nothing to offer, Jesus says, have the most.

In other words, you must be broken to be made whole.

This week, we're looking at Jesus's second beatitude:

BLESSED ARE THOSE WHO MOURN, FOR THEY WILL BE
COMFORTED

- MATTHEW 5:4

Remember that these blessings are not unconnected. Jesus's blessings are on a single group of people who the world has rejected, a multifaceted family of people who seem *less than*.

So, there's continuity between the poor in spirit and those who mourn. This week, we'll look at "those who mourn," the down and out, why they are blessed in this upside-down economy of Jesus, and why he promises them comfort.

WHEN DREAMS COME TO AN END

So who are those who mourn? They are those who have awakened to the reality of life and discovered it to be painful, unjust, and irrevocably broken.

The mourners have come to the end of themselves by suffering loss. "But," you might say, "I haven't really lost someone or something, and I'm still sad." But if we are defining loss as only death, we have only gotten a portion of the picture. Loss is everywhere; it's a part of life.

Kyle writes,
"The end of me often comes when my dreams come to an end. Maybe for you it was pretty early on, when your mom and dad sat you down and introduced you to the word *divorce*. Maybe it was a message from the person you thought was "the one," telling you it just wasn't going to work out. Perhaps it was a phone call telling you there had been an accident and you needed to come to the hospital." (42)

The list could go on and on, forever. The losses in this life seem endless. "If you're going to live, you're going to lose. You will come to the end of yourself." (43)

When our dreams come to an end, when we suffer loss, we hurt. We grieve. We become sad, and not the kind of sad that goes away with a quick laugh or chocolate chip cookie.

No, when our dreams come to an end, when we enter the real world of pain and loss, we become "those who mourn."

But there's good news.

GOOD NEWS FOR THE MOURNERS

The good news is that those who mourn will not do so forever. "Blessed are those who mourn," Jesus says to all of us who mourn sickness, family breakdown, generational sin, and injustice in the world. "For they will be comforted."

Could it be?

Those who mourn, Jesus seems to be saying, have special access to the Lord's healing power. Those who mourn get a direct line to the God who is present.

And much as it is with the poor in spirit, those who mourn have something in common with Christ himself. Jesus, it was said, was a Man of Sorrows.

When Jesus saw the brokenness of Jerusalem, "he wept over it" (Luke 19:41).

When Lazarus died, Jesus "shuddered with emotion and deeply moved with tenderness and compassion" (John 11:33, The Passion Translation), and "he wept" (John 11:35).

When he retreated to the Garden of Gethsemane, Jesus "began to be sorrowful and troubled" and said, "My soul is overwhelmed with sorrow to the point of death" (Matthew 26:37-38).

For now, consider that if you are sad, if you mourn the death of a friend, if you grieve over the brokenness of the world, you are not alone.

Among "those who mourn" is Jesus himself.

NOW WHEN JESUS SAW THE CROWDS, HE WENT UP ON A MOUNTAINSIDE AND SAT DOWN. AND HE BEGAN TO TEACH THEM. HE SAID: BLESSED ARE THE POOR IN SPIRIT, FOR THEIRS IS THE KINGDOM OF HEAVEN. BLESSED ARE THOSE WHO MOURN, FOR THEY WILL BE COMFORTED."
- MATTHEW 5:1-4

CONTENT AND MEANING

WHO IS JESUS DESCRIBING WHEN HE REFERS TO "THOSE WHO MOURN"? WHO IS INCLUDED IN THIS GROUP? IS ANYONE EXCLUDED?

WHAT IS THE CONNECTION BETWEEN THE POOR IN SPIRIT AND THOSE WHO MOURN? WHAT OVERLAPPING TRAITS OR EXPERIENCES DO THEY SHARE?

WHY DO YOU THINK JESUS USES HIS SECOND BEATITUDE ON THOSE WHO MOURN?

MEDITATION AND APPLICATION

READ MATTHEW 5:1-4 AGAIN SLOWLY AND ANSWER THE FOLLOWING QUESTIONS.

IN WHAT WAYS DO YOU IDENTIFY WITH THE MOURNERS? IN WHAT WAYS DO YOU STRUGGLE TO IDENTIFY AS ONE WHO MOURNS?

HOW DO YOU RESPOND TO THE SCRIPTURES THAT DESCRIBE JESUS'S SORROWFUL EMOTIONS?

EXERCISE

WE WILL BE DISCUSSING GRIEF AND LOSS THROUGHOUT THIS WEEK'S STUDY. TAKE A FEW MINUTES TODAY TO MAKE A LIST OF PAINFUL LOSSES YOU HAVE EXPERIENCED. KEEPING THESE LOSSES IN MIND THROUGHOUT THESE DEVOTIONAL STUDIES WILL ENABLE YOU TO APPROACH PRAYER AND REFLECTION MORE FULLY. WHEN SPECIFIC LOSSES ARE ON YOUR MIND, IT OPENS YOU UP TO TRANSFORMATION.

CONSIDER DIFFERENT SEASONS OF LIFE: CHILDHOOD, ADOLESCENCE, EARLY ADULTHOOD, MIDLIFE, LATE ADULTHOOD

CONSIDER VARIOUS RELATIONSHIPS: YOUR PARENTS, CHILDHOOD FRIENDS, DATING RELATIONSHIPS, MARRIAGE, PARENTING, ADULT FRIENDSHIPS, WORKPLACE RELATIONSHIPS

CONSIDER OTHER FORMS OF LOSS: GETTING LET GO FROM A JOB OR MISSING A PROMOTION, LOSING THE ABILITY TO DO SOMETHING YOU LOVE, MISSING A PREVIOUS SEASON OF LIFE

mourning our circumstances

W e live in a broken world, and in a broken world, there is much to mourn.

We mourn our circumstances—our failing health, a broken relationship, a lost job or missed promotion, or the death of a loved one.

We mourn our sin—our inability to do the good that we intend, our rebellion against the laws of God, our preference for the broad, easy path of life.

And we mourn the brokenness of our world—the result of our sin and others' sin. Our world is gripped by injustices including poverty and racism, and by natural disasters like hurricanes, tsunamis, and tornados.

There is, indeed, much to make us sorrowful. So it comes as a shock when Jesus says,

BLESSED ARE THOSE WHO MOURN, FOR THEY WILL BE COMFORTED

- MATTHEW 5:4

Today, we're asking: What does it mean to mourn our circumstances, and how do we find Jesus's blessing here?

HAVE YOU CONSIDERED JOB?

The suffering of Job is one of the most well-known stories in the Old Testament.

The book of Job is perhaps the earliest biblical account we have. Experts believe Job lived in the period before Abraham, Isaac, and Jacob.

If anyone had reason to mourn his circumstances, it was Job.

The prologue to Job reads like a Hall of Fame induction ceremony. Job was probably the wealthiest person in the world. "He was the greatest man among all the people of the East" (Job 1:3). He made sacrifices for his own sin and even his children's sin. In God's words, "There is no one on earth like him; he is blameless and upright, a man who fears God and shuns evil" (1:8).

Suddenly, Job experiences profound loss. His circumstances go from unbelievably great to shockingly awful in short time. And here's the most disturbing part: God doesn't just *allow* Job's suffering, he seems to *suggest* it.

One day, Scripture says, Satan approaches God in heaven after his usual threatening and evil work on earth. God asks Satan, "Have you considered my servant Job?"

Initially, Satan scoffs at Job's righteousness, suggesting surely Job is only faithful because of his great circumstances. So the Lord permits Satan to bring harm into Job's life: "Everything he has is in your power, but on the man himself do not lay a finger" (1:12).

So Satan goes off to his evil work. In a single day, Job's fortune of oxen and donkeys are destroyed by the Sabeans, his sheep are burned by a fire, and his camels are killed by the Chaldeans (1:13-17). And in the same day, Job's beloved children are killed in a tornado (1:18-19).

In just one day, Job loses almost everything: his sons, his daughters, his servants, and his possessions. He is stripped of it all. And yet, even still, the text records: "In all this, Job did not sin by charging God with wrongdoing" (1:22).

But the losses don't end there: Sometime later, Job's health is taken from him, and he is covered in painful sores from head to toe (2:4-8). And his wife, perhaps his last joy and consolation in life, ridicules him, and urges him to curse God and die (2:5-9). And still, "In all this, Job did not sin" (2:10).

How on earth could an individual survive all this suffering?

GOD IN THE STORM

Over the following forty chapters of the book, Job wrestles with God. He asks, why? His friends try to make sense of his loss and offer counsel. But it's the presence of God that gets Job through.

Kyle writes:
"In surprising ways, suffering makes room in our spirit for us to know and experience the blessing of God's peace and presence. Without suffering, we simply can't know his comfort. In mourning, we experience the blessing of God's presence." (49)

Job entered the darkness. He was swept up in the storm of the world's brokenness. He suffered in ways few of us (probably none of us) will ever experience. And yet, there was a blessing in the darkness.

In Job's great grief and confusion, "the LORD spoke to Job out of the storm" (38:1). God's response to Job's losses is not what we expect: Over five chapters, God recounts his complete control over the universe. But it's not bragging, and it's not cruelty. It's comfort. God is in complete control over every bird in the air, every planet in the sky, and every ounce of dirt in the ground, so surely he is capable of comforting Job in his pain.

After God's hurricane appearance, Job can only respond: "My ears had heard of you. But now my eyes have seen you" (42:5).

When God comes in the storm, we experience him in a profound, new way.

There's a gift in the darkness, a blessing in the storm. The blessing is God himself.

Kyle concludes:
"Here's what we find in our suffering. There is a deep void that used to be filled with whatever we lost. That could be stuff or even relationships—none of which are bad things. But when it's gone, it leaves an aching cavity, and God is there to fill it up with himself.

"When we suffer, we mourn. When we mourn, we are comforted by 'the God of all comfort' (2 Cor. 1:3). *Blessed* are those who mourn." (50)

SCRIPTURE MEMORY

 NOW WHEN JESUS SAW THE CROWDS, HE WENT UP ON A MOUNTAINSIDE AND SAT DOWN. AND HE BEGAN TO TEACH THEM. HE SAID: BLESSED ARE THE POOR IN SPIRIT, FOR THEIRS IS THE KINGDOM OF HEAVEN. BLESSED ARE THOSE WHO MOURN, FOR THEY WILL BE COMFORTED."   - MATTHEW 5:1-4

CONTENT AND MEANING

READ JOB 1-2 AND 38-42. HOW WOULD YOU SUMMARIZE THE MESSAGE OF THE BOOK?

WHAT NEW REFLECTIONS OR QUESTIONS HAVE SURFACED THROUGH YOUR STUDY OF JOB'S LIFE AND LOSSES?

WHAT TYPES OF SUFFERING DO YOU THINK JESUS'S ORIGINAL HEARERS IN MATTHEW 5 WOULD HAVE BEEN EXPERIENCING?

MEDITATION AND APPLICATION

READ MATTHEW 5:1-4 AGAIN SLOWLY AND ANSWER THE FOLLOWING QUESTIONS.

EVEN IF YOUR LOSSES HAVE NOT BEEN AS SUDDEN AND DRAMATIC, WE CAN FIND OUR SUFFERING IN THE STORY OF JOB. IN WHAT WAYS DO YOU RESONATE WITH JOB'S STORY?

HAVE YOU EVER RECEIVED BAD COUNSEL WHILE SUFFERING? HOW DID IT MAKE YOU FEEL?

HOW DO YOU RESPOND TO KYLE'S STATEMENT THAT OUR SUFFERING REVEALS "A DEEP VOID THAT USED TO BE FILLED WITH WHATEVER WE LOST... AND GOD IS THERE TO FILL IT UP WITH HIMSELF"? HOW HAVE YOU EXPERIENCED THIS PERSONALLY?

EXERCISE

FINISH THE FOLLOWING SENTENCES BY JOURNALING FOR A FEW SENTENCES:

GOD WILL NOT WASTE MY PAIN, BECAUSE

GOD WILL NOT LEAVE ME ALONE, BECAUSE

mourning our sin

n our broken world, there is much to mourn. Yesterday, we discussed the need to mourn our circumstances—declining health, broken relationships, losing loved ones, and other pains.

In Job's life, we saw a man who had it all and lost it all. Yet in his loss, he gained something new: He experienced God directly.

When we lose something we love, whether a person or a possession, there's an opportunity to have the void filled by God's own presence.

Today, we continue to look at Jesus's blessing to "those who mourn" (Matthew 5:4). But today, we consider how to mourn our *sin*.

In mourning our sin, we also discover God's mercy and find a hidden strength for life in our broken world.

WHY WE (STILL) TALK ABOUT SIN

In *The End of Me*, Kyle Idleman notes that the word *sin* is slowly being lost from our modern vocabulary. While the Greek New Testament uses 33 different words for sin, our culture generally wants to avoid the term and idea altogether (55).

But we need to keep sin in our vocabulary. Why? "Without seeing the depths of sin, we'll never understand the heights of God's love and grace" (57).

David's prayer in Psalm 32 is a case study of how mourning our sin produces a deep awareness of God's forgiveness and grants strength for this life.

WHEN I KEPT SILENT, MY BONES WASTED AWAYTHROUGH MY GROANING ALL DAY

LONG. FOR DAY AND NIGHT
YOUR HAND WAS HEAVY ON ME;
MY STRENGTH WAS SAPPED AS IN
THE HEAT OF SUMMER. THEN I
ACKNOWLEDGED MY SIN TO YOU AND
DID NOT COVER UP MY INIQUITY. I SAID,
"I WILL CONFESS MY TRANSGRESSIONS
TO THE LORD." AND YOU FORGAVE THE
GUILT OF MY SIN.

- PSALM 32:3-5

Instead of denying or minimizing our sin, we would do well to bring it directly to light. When we "keep silent," our sin corrupts our souls. Our hearts become heavy. Our bodies cry out. We simply can't handle the guilt and shame of the hidden sin.

Where sin is hidden, it remains powerful. It stays in control.

Where sin is revealed, it loses power. It gives up control.

WHEN LIGHT SHINES IN THE DARKNESS, AND THE DARKNESS
CANNOT OVERCOME IT.

- JOHN 1:5

Kyle writes,
"Seeing myself in painful perspective allows me to rejoice in full fidelity. I know how great God's mercy is, because I know how little I deserve it. The deeper my mourning, the greater a party I need to throw, because something miraculous has happened." (57)

The false promise of sin is that it will liberate us. It won't. It will only oppress us and hold us in bondage until Christ comes and breaks the chains. Apart from Christ, our sin brings only guilt and shame.

But Christ—now don't miss this—took our sin to the Cross and paid its penalty of death in full. Yes, our sin cost Jesus his life. But Christ's death was also victory over sin.

On the third day, Jesus rose from the dead in complete victory over sin and its co-conspirators, the devil and death. Sin could not keep Jesus in the grave. Our sin is no longer held against us.

It's now *our* sin in the grave, and Christ is seated on the Throne!

MOURNING OUR SIN AND GLADNESS

It's because of God's forgiveness—ultimately through Christ on the Cross—that Psalm 32 can conclude with joy and gladness.

> REJOICE IN THE LORD AND BE GLAD, YOU RIGHTEOUS;
> SING, ALL YOU WHO ARE UPRIGHT IN HEART!

> - PSALM 32:11

This is the paradox: Mourning is the path to blessing. Acknowledging sin opens us to the joy of grace.

We must mourn our sin to be truly happy.

SCRIPTURE MEMORY

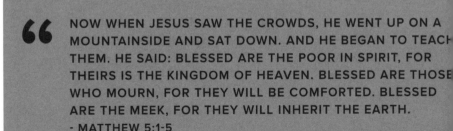

NOW WHEN JESUS SAW THE CROWDS, HE WENT UP ON A MOUNTAINSIDE AND SAT DOWN. AND HE BEGAN TO TEACH THEM. HE SAID: BLESSED ARE THE POOR IN SPIRIT, FOR THEIRS IS THE KINGDOM OF HEAVEN. BLESSED ARE THOSE WHO MOURN, FOR THEY WILL BE COMFORTED. BLESSED ARE THE MEEK, FOR THEY WILL INHERIT THE EARTH.
- MATTHEW 5:1-5

WHERE SIN IS REVEALED, IT LOSES POWER. IT GIVES UP CONTROL.

CONTENT AND MEANING

READ PSALM 32 IN ITS ENTIRETY. WHICH VERSES OR LINES STAND OUT TO YOU THE MOST?

HOW WOULD ONE READ PSALM 32 IN ITS ORIGINAL CONTEXT—IN ISRAEL, BEFORE THE MESSIAH? HOW DOES KNOWLEDGE OF JESUS'S LIFE, DEATH, AND RESURRECTION CHANGE THE WAY YOU READ IT?

QUESTIONS FOR REFLECTION

MEDITATION AND APPLICATION

READ MATTHEW 5:1-5 AGAIN SLOWLY AND ANSWER THE FOLLOWING QUESTIONS.

REFLECT ON A TIME WHEN YOU TRIED TO CONCEAL OR MINIMIZE YOUR SIN. HOW DID IT FEEL?

CAN YOU THINK OF ANY HIDDEN SIN THAT REMAINS? WHAT WOULD IT LOOK LIKE TO BRING THAT SIN INTO THE LIGHT, SO THAT IT LOSES POWER (JOHN 1:5)?

REMEMBER KYLE'S STATEMENT FROM YESTERDAY: MOURNING REVEALS "A DEEP VOID THAT USED TO BE FILLED WITH WHATEVER WE LOST... AND GOD IS THERE TO FILL IT UP WITH HIMSELF"? HOW DO YOU THINK THIS COULD BE TRUE OF MOURNING YOUR OWN SIN?

blessed are the hungry

When we lose something we love, whether a person or a possession, we mourn the loss. But in the emptiness of loss, there's an opportunity to have the void filled by God's presence.

The past two days, we looked at mourning our circumstances and mourning our sin. Today, we move from Jesus's second beatitude to his fourth, but we'll discover significant continuity. Jesus says:

> BLESSED ARE THOSE WHO HUNGER AND THIRST FOR RIGHTEOUSNESS, FOR THEY WILL BE FILLED.
>
> - MATTHEW 5:6

In mourning our sin, we discover God's mercy and find a hidden strength for life in our broken world. In our hunger and thirst for righteousness, we find that God is enough and that he alone fills our needs.

WHO HUNGERS FOR RIGHTEOUSNESS?

The first three beatitudes—blessed are the poor in spirit, those who mourn, the meek—comfort us in our weakness. But to *hunger and thirst for righteousness* is more active. Jesus is offering praise and congratulations to those who are in hot pursuit of the truly Good Life.

The "righteousness" described here is not the definitive gift of right standing as Paul uses it in his letters to the Romans and Galatians. Instead, in the Gospels, "righteousness" refers to an overarching degree of goodness, right conduct, and Christ-like character.

and thirsty

Those who hunger and thirst for righteousness want to be like Christ, want to be good, and want to do right. But they have not yet attained that which they seek. It is not "Blessed are the righteous" but "Blessed are those who *hunger and thirst for righteousness.*"

One commentator summarizes this beatitude well:

> **"The hungry-for-righteousness are blessed… because they feel starved for and empty of a needed righteousness. Jesus does not bless those conscious of their righteousness or victorious life. Rather, God's promise is given to people for whom righteousness, victory, vindication, and right conduct seem painfully missing, in themselves and in others. [These] Beatitudes are not celebrations of high self-esteem."**

So, the hungry and thirsty, like the poor in spirit and those who mourn, are characterized by *need*.

They *need* righteousness.
They *need* justice.
They *need* God's victory.
They *need* all Jesus has too.

To be hungry and thirsty is a matter of life and death. Like we need food and drink, we need righteousness. We long and stagger in thirst for the ways and laws of the Lord.

THEY WILL BE FILLED

The hungry and thirsty are characterized by their need, and Jesus promises to cover their plates and fill their cups to the brim. "For they will be filled."

What are you hungry and thirsty for? What do you long for? What do you *want*?

When we align our wants and needs with the ways of Jesus, there's a blessing. When we want what he wants and need what he provides, the promise holds for us.

In the same speech as these beatitudes, Jesus teaches his disciples to pray: "Thy kingdom come; thy will be done, on earth as it is in heaven" (Matthew 6:10).

This is the heart cry, the deep hunger and thirst, of those who receive Jesus's blessing: May your kingdom grow—not mine! May your heavenly will reach down to earth!

Indeed, there is great continuity: The poor in spirit have come to the end of themselves. Those who mourn look to God to fill their loss. The hungry and thirsty long for the righteous life of Christ.

In the upside-down kingdom, it's more blessed to lack than to have. The hungry and thirsty know this: They are begging for more of God and less of themselves.

And what does Jesus say? *They will be filled.*

SCRIPTURE MEMORY
REVIEW MATTHEW 5:1-6

CONTENT AND MEANING

WHAT IS THE CONNECTION BETWEEN THE FIRST THREE
BEATITUDES AND THE FOURTH?

HOW DOES THIS BEATITUDE CHALLENGE THE CONVENTIONAL
WISDOM AND WAYS OF OUR WORLD?

HOW WOULD SOMEONE ALIGN THEIR DESIRES WITH JESUS'S
DESIRES?

QUESTIONS FOR REFLECTION

MEDITATION AND APPLICATION

READ MATTHEW 5:1-6 AGAIN SLOWLY AND THEN READ PSALM 34:8-10 BELOW AND REFLECT ON THE FOLLOWING QUESTIONS.

TASTE AND SEE THAT THE LORD IS GOOD; BLESSED IS THE ONE WHO TAKES REFUGE IN HIM. FEAR THE LORD, YOU HIS HOLY PEOPLE, FOR THOSE WHO FEAR HIM LACK NOTHING. THE LIONS MAY GROW WEAK AND HUNGRY, BUT THOSE WHO SEEK THE LORD LACK NO GOOD THING.

WHAT DOES IT MEAN FOR YOU TO "TASTE AND SEE THAT THE LORD IS GOOD"? HOW IS THIS LIKE OR UNLIKE HUNGERING AND THIRSTING FOR RIGHTEOUSNESS?

HOW DOES IT COMFORT YOU THAT THOSE WHO LOVE AND FOLLOW GOD WILL "LACK NOTHING," WILL "LACK NO GOOD THING"?

WHAT WOULD IT LOOK LIKE FOR YOU TO PURSUE
RIGHTEOUSNESS—TO REALLY HUNGER AND THIRST AFTER
IT—TODAY?

FINALLY, READ PSALM 34'S PROMISES TO THE RIGHTEOUS.
HOW DO YOU SEE THESE PROMISES FORESHADOW
JESUS'S BEATITUDES?

THE EYES OF THE LORD ARE ON THE
RIGHTEOUS

- PSALM 34:15

THE RIGHTEOUS CRY OUT, AND THE LORD
HEARS THEM

- PSALM 34:17

THE RIGHTEOUS PERSON MAY HAVE TROUBLES,
BUT THE LORD DELIVERS HIM FROM THEM ALL

- PSALM 34:19

the Lord of sorrows

We have recently looked at the second and fourth Beatitudes:

BLESSED ARE THOSE WHO MOURN,
FOR THEY WILL BE COMFORTED.
BLESSED ARE THOSE WHO HUNGER AND THIRST FOR RIGHTEOUSNESS,
FOR THEY WILL BE FILLED.

- MATTHEW 5:4, 6

In mourning our sin, we discover God's mercy and find a hidden strength for life in our broken world. In our hunger and thirst for righteousness, we find that God is enough and that he alone fills our need.

Notice the connection: Those who mourn have a hole in their hearts that only God can fill. Those who hunger and thirst for righteousness will settle for nothing less than God's filling.

Where there's a need, God provides. Where there's pain, God comforts. Where there's pain, whether from loss or hunger, Jesus arrives.

JESUS WEPT

Jesus was a man of sorrows, acquainted with grief. He was no stranger to loss and didn't have to speak of pain and suffering in general terms. He felt it. He hurt. He wept.

One day, Jesus was ministering to his disciples when their friend, Mary, approached him with bad news. Lazarus, Mary's brother and Jesus's close friend, was dangerously sick. John 11 notes that Jesus loved Lazarus, and Mary and her sister, Martha (v. 5).

But surprisingly, Jesus doesn't leave right away. He waits several days, and then finally makes the trip to see Lazarus. Along the way, Martha greets Jesus with bad news and an accusation: Lazarus is dead, and you could have saved him!

Maybe you resonate with this. Why does the Lord not answer me right away? Why do my prayers seem to go unanswered? Why does the Lord seem absent when I need him most? I thought he loved me!

But still, Jesus comes to see Lazarus. The text says he is "deeply moved in spirit and troubled" (John 11:33). That phrase in the original Greek means something like upset in his stomach, groaning in pain, or overwhelmed with grief. Seeing Lazarus's family members grieve, Jesus begins to weep (v. 35).

We see, in Christ, the most loyal, compassionate and loving Man who ever lived. He was fully human and wasn't afraid to weep openly at the death of a friend. In his tears, we find that our pain, our sadness over death are not foreign to him. To be fully human is to mourn and grieve deeply. We live in a world wrecked by sin and death, and at our core, we are restless and weary with suffering.

Jesus fulfilled the words of the prophet Isaiah,

> HE WAS DESPISED AND REJECTED BY MEN,
> A MAN OF SORROWS AND ACQUAINTED WITH GRIEF.
>
> - ISAIAH 53:3

He was acquainted with grief, but not overcome by it. He is not the Lord of death but life.

LORD OF DEATH AND LIFE

Speaking to the crowd that had gathered at Lazarus's tomb, Jesus says, "I am the resurrection and the life. The one who believes in me will live, even though they die; and whoever lives by believing in me will never die" (v. 25-26).

Then turning to the tomb, Jesus calls out in a loud voice, "Lazarus, come out!" (v. 43). And then the unthinkable happened: "The dead man came out, his hands and feet wrapped with strips of linen, and a cloth around his face" (v. 44). And before the speechless crowd, Jesus says, "Take off the grave clothes and let him go" (v. 45).

Jesus is the resurrection and the life. Whoever believes in him will live—even though we die.

In Christ, we have a man of sorrows, acquainted with grief. He is no stranger to loss; he knows our pains. But he knew that death was not the end. There is a hope beyond the grave.

Jesus knows that we will mourn in this life, but we will be comforted in this life and in the one to come. Even though our world is full of loss, pain, grief, and death—all things he personally experienced—he is greater still.

This is the paradox: In death, there is life. In suffering, there is glory. In hunger and thirst, there is satisfaction. In mourning, there is comfort.

SCRIPTURE MEMORY

NOW WHEN JESUS SAW THE CROWDS, HE WENT UP ON A MOUNTAINSIDE AND SAT DOWN. AND HE BEGAN TO TEACH THEM. HE SAID: BLESSED ARE THE POOR IN SPIRIT, FOR THEIRS IS THE KINGDOM OF HEAVEN. BLESSED ARE THOSE WHO MOURN, FOR THEY WILL BE COMFORTED. BLESSED ARE THE MEEK, FOR THEY WILL INHERIT THE EARTH. BLESSED ARE THOSE WHO HUNGER AND THIRST FOR RIGHTEOUSNESS, FOR THEY WILL BE FILLED.
- MATTHEW 5:1-6

CONTENT AND MEANING

READ JOHN 11 IN ITS ENTIRETY. WHICH PARTS OF THE STORY SURPRISE YOU MOST?

THINK THROUGH THE STORIES AND EVENTS OF THE GOSPELS. HOW MANY EMOTIONS DO YOU SEE IN JESUS? HOW DOES THIS CHANGE THE WAY YOU THINK ABOUT HIM?

WHY CAN JESUS SAY TO US TODAY: "THE ONE WHO BELIEVES IN ME WILL LIVE, EVEN THOUGH THEY DIE" (JOHN 11:25)?

MEDITATION AND APPLICATION

READ MATTHEW 5:1-6 AGAIN SLOWLY AND ANSWER THE FOLLOWING QUESTION.

THINK OF A TIME YOU EXPERIENCED LOSS AND GRIEF—WHEN YOU CAME TO THE END OF YOURSELF. HOW DID JESUS MEET YOU THERE? HOW DID YOU EXPERIENCE HIM AS "A MAN OF SORROWS, ACQUAINTED WITH GRIEF"?

the opposite of mourning

Everyone loves to laugh. A good joke makes us smile, and an unexpected smile brightens our day.

But too often we laugh at the wrong things. We smirk at inappropriate humor. We laugh at the failure or hurt of another—this was the entire premise of *America's Funniest Home Videos*. But when true suffering appears on our TV screen, we want to change the channel.

Mourning and laughter seem like opposites. But are they really?

Kyle writes on page 59 in *The End of Me*:

> **"There is a joy and peace that come only when we finally let ourselves see the sin and let our eyes shed tears for it. Because in the midst of all those tears, all that grief, is where God's blessing can be found…. There is no way to get to that blessing without the mourning that precedes it."**

Perhaps it could be that mourning and laughter are connected—but not in the way we initially think.

We must begin by turning our laughter into mourning.

TURN YOUR LAUGHTER INTO MOURNING

Here's how the apostle James puts it:

> COME NEAR
> TO GOD AND
> HE WILL COME
> NEAR TO YOU.
> WASH YOUR
> HANDS, YOU
> SINNERS, AND
> PURIFY YOUR
> HEARTS, YOU

DOUBLE-MINDED. GRIEVE, MOURN AND WAIL. CHANGE YOUR LAUGHTER TO MOURNING AND YOUR JOY TO GLOOM. HUMBLE YOURSELVES BEFORE THE LORD, AND HE WILL LIFT YOU UP.

-JAMES 4:8-9

Our world is broken, and to be like Christ, we must stare directly into the eyes of the world's pain.

Similarly, Ecclesiastes 7:3 says,

FRUSTRATION IS BETTER THAN LAUGHTER, BECAUSE A SAD FACE IS GOOD FOR THE HEART.

And Proverbs 14:13 says,

EVEN IN LAUGHTER THE HEART MAY ACHE, AND REJOICING MAY END IN GRIEF.

While we want lighthearted and silly, our world is heavy and painful.

If we want joy—true, lasting happiness, and peace in Christ—then we must not always look away from the hurt. We must enter into mourning. We must grieve. We must be okay with a deep sadness.

This may sound awful, but remember, there's a blessing in the brokenness. The way of the Kingdom is not the way of the world.

Down is up, weak is strong, and tears bring healing.

WHEN MOURNING TURNS (BACK) TO LAUGHTER

Yes, mourning and laughter are connected—but not in the way we initially think. It turns out that it's our mourning that *enables* laughter.

"Mourning is true and focused grief, just you and God, and it's often marked by tears.... You'll have to walk through the valley of the shadow, but I promise you this: you'll never walk alone" (Idleman 62)

Mourning brings us to the end of ourselves.

And as Kyle writes, "At the end of me is singing and rejoicing!" (60)

SCRIPTURE MEMORY

NOW WHEN JESUS SAW THE CROWDS, HE WENT UP ON A MOUNTAINSIDE AND SAT DOWN. AND HE BEGAN TO TEACH THEM. HE SAID: BLESSED ARE THE POOR IN SPIRIT, FOR THEIRS IS THE KINGDOM OF HEAVEN. BLESSED ARE THOSE WHO MOURN, FOR THEY WILL BE COMFORTED. BLESSED ARE THE MEEK, FOR THEY WILL INHERIT THE EARTH. BLESSED ARE THOSE WHO HUNGER AND THIRST FOR RIGHTEOUSNESS, FOR THEY WILL BE FILLED. BLESSED ARE THE MERCIFUL, FOR THEY WILL BE SHOWN MERCY.

- MATTHEW 5:1-7

EXERCISE

Let's close today with the exercise Kyle recommends on pages 61-62 in *The End of Me*. Consider the Old Testament tradition called penitential mourning. This form of grief was a focused, defined time for the whole community to grieve together.

WHAT IN YOUR LIFE NEEDS TO BE MOURNED? CONSIDER THE FOLLOWING QUESTIONS FROM PAGE 61.

HOW HAVE I SINNED IN THE LAST FEW DAYS?

WHO ELSE HAS BEEN HURT BY MY SIN?

BESIDES CONFESSING TO GOD, IS THERE SOMEONE I NEED TO APOLOGIZE TO?

HOW CAN I CLEAN UP THE MESS MY SIN MADE?

WHOM WILL I CONFESS MY SINS TO?

WHAT EXCUSES AND JUSTIFICATIONS HAVE I JUST COME UP WITH IN ANSWERING THESE QUESTIONS?

CONTENT AND MEANING

WHAT IS THE PRIMARY CONNECTION BETWEEN LAUGHTER AND MOURNING IN THE SCRIPTURES?

HOW DOES PSALM 32 (SEE DAY 10) RELATE TO THE SCRIPTURE PASSAGES WE READ TODAY?

QUESTIONS FOR REFLECTION

MEDITATION AND APPLICATION

READ MATTHEW 5:1-5 AGAIN SLOWLY AND ANSWER THE FOLLOWING QUESTIONS.

WHERE DID YOU FEEL YOURSELF RESISTING TODAY'S DEVOTIONAL MESSAGE? WHERE DO YOU SENSE RESISTANCE TO THE IDEA OF LETTING YOURSELF MOURN AND GRIEVE?

WHERE IS IT EASIEST FOR YOU TO MOURN: YOUR CIRCUMSTANCES, YOUR SIN, OR THE BROKENNESS OF THE WORLD? WHY DO YOU THINK THAT IS?

REFLECTION & REVIEW

O n the seventh day of each week, we're going to pause to review and reflect on the past week.

If you are behind a day or two, use this day to catch up.

If you are caught up, use this day to review the previous six days' notes—especially all the Scripture references and stories. Use these seventh days to review your Scripture memory verses as well.

SCRIPTURE MEMORY

REVIEW MATTHEW 5:1-7

NOW WHEN JESUS SAW THE CROWDS, HE WENT UP ON A MOUNTAINSIDE AND SAT DOWN. AND HE BEGAN TO TEACH THEM. HE SAID: BLESSED ARE THE POOR IN SPIRIT, FOR THEIRS IS THE KINGDOM OF HEAVEN. BLESSED ARE THOSE WHO MOURN, FOR THEY WILL BE COMFORTED. BLESSED ARE THE MEEK, FOR THEY WILL INHERIT THE EARTH. BLESSED ARE THOSE WHO HUNGER AND THIRST FOR RIGHTEOUSNESS, FOR THEY WILL BE FILLED. BLESSED ARE THE MERCIFUL, FOR THEY WILL BE SHOWN MERCY.

QUESTIONS FOR REFLECTION

BASED ON YOUR WEEK'S READING AND
REFLECTION, ANSWER THE FOLLOWING
QUESTIONS.

WHAT WAS THE MOST SIGNIFICANT THING I
LEARNED ABOUT JESUS AND THE CHRISTIAN
LIFE THIS WEEK?

WHAT WAS THE MOST SIGNIFICANT THING I
LEARNED ABOUT MOURNING THIS WEEK?

WHAT WAS THE MOST SIGNIFICANT THING I LEARNED ABOUT MYSELF THIS WEEK?

WHAT WOULD MY LIFE LOOK LIKE IF I FULLY BELIEVED AND LIVED EVERYTHING I READ AND WROTE THIS WEEK?

AUTHENTIC TO BE ACCEPTED

Blessed are the pure in heart,
for they will see God.

Matthew 5:8

THREE

the pure in heart

Jesus is quick to blow up our expectations.

Let's review.

EVERYTHING IS UPSIDE DOWN

In his Sermon on the Mount, Jesus teaches that the truly Good Life is not the one full of comfort, stability, acceptance, and status. Counterintuitively, Jesus says, it is blessed to be poor. Blessed to mourn. Blessed to be hungry and thirsty. Blessed to be pure and merciful. Blessed even to be rejected and persecuted.

Jesus opens his Sermon—a sort of new law for the new people of God—with a series of blessings, called beatitudes. In the Beatitudes, everything is upside down. Brokenness is the way to wholeness. Mourning is the way to happiness. Authenticity is the way to acceptance. And emptiness is the way to fullness.

Everything is upside down, according to Jesus.

He longs to turn your world right-side up.

True blessedness isn't found in looking within ourselves or developing self-esteem. The Good Life isn't found by focusing on me at all. Instead, blessedness is found in less of me and more of Christ.

The Good Life comes only at the end of me. When you come to the end of me, you are free to live as Christ intended—free to be truly blessed.

As we have seen, you must be broken to be whole, and you must mourn to be happy. This week, we'll discover another reality of the upside-down kingdom:

You must be authentic to be accepted. Let's begin our next journey with an important question.

DO YOU KNOW YOUR HEART?

How well do you know your heart?

We know that biologically speaking, our heart is the lumpy red organ that pumps blood around and keeps us alive. In everyday language, we refer to our "heart" as our emotions, our feelings, or our desires. We say, "He broke my heart!" Or maybe, "She has a lot of heart!" Or even, "What a heartless thing to do!"

But in the Scriptures, the heart has an even deeper function than survival and feeling.

In biblical use, your "heart" is the very core of your being, that which drives your motivations, orders your life, and guides your decisions.

As Oswald Chambers wrote,

> **"According to the Bible, the heart is the center: The center of physical life, the center of mercy, the center of damnation and salvation, the center of God's working and the devil's working and the center from which everything works which molds the human mechanism...**
>
> **"The heart is not merely the seat of affections, it is the center of everything. The heart is the central altar and the body is the outer court. What we offer on the altar of the heart will ultimately tell through the extremities of the body."**

Your heart is your center; it moves everything from your feelings to your thoughts and your decisions. The question is: What's going on in your heart?

THE PURE IN HEART

Jesus's fifth beatitude is a powerful one:

> BLESSED ARE THE PURE IN HEART, FOR THEY WILL SEE GOD.
>
> - MATTHEW 5:8

Who are "the pure in heart"? Most simply: If our hearts are the center of our beings, the pure in heart are those who are pure at their center.

We often think of purity as being an *external* cleanness—someone who doesn't break laws, do drugs, or engage in sexual immorality. In the first century, Jesus's original listeners had viewed purity in this way. God's people were to be pure, clean, and unstained by the world. They did their best to show one another that they ate the right foods, wore the right clothes, and acted right in public.

But Jesus puts a spin on it: Blessed are the pure *in heart*.

Jesus is saying: It's not the outside that matters. It's not what you eat, what you wear, or what you do in public. It's not what others say about you. It's what's on the inside that matters.

The kind of purity Jesus blesses is a *purity of heart*—a purity that begins in the very core of our being, a purity that drives all of our feelings, thoughts, and decisions.

Blessed are the pure in heart.

Kyle writes:

"It means you're living the blessed life when you stop worrying about the signs and the extravagant advertising and all the effort expended trying to convince people you're something different than you are. When the inside and outside match up, you're pure in heart and you're where he wants you to be.

"Getting to the end of me means I'm not worried about performing for others anymore." (91)

SCRIPTURE MEMORY

NOW WHEN JESUS SAW THE CROWDS, HE WENT UP ON A MOUNTAINSIDE AND SAT DOWN. AND HE BEGAN TO TEACH THEM. HE SAID: BLESSED ARE THE POOR IN SPIRIT, FOR THEIRS IS THE KINGDOM OF HEAVEN. BLESSED ARE THOSE WHO MOURN, FOR THEY WILL BE COMFORTED. BLESSED ARE THE MEEK, FOR THEY WILL INHERIT THE EARTH. BLESSED ARE THOSE WHO HUNGER AND THIRST FOR RIGHTEOUSNESS, FOR THEY WILL BE FILLED. BLESSED ARE THE MERCIFUL, FOR THEY WILL BE SHOWN MERCY. BLESSED ARE THE PURE IN HEART, FOR THEY WILL SEE GOD.

- MATTHEW 5:1-8

QUESTIONS FOR REFLECTION

CONTENT AND MEANING

ACCORDING TO THE SCRIPTURES, WHAT IS THE MEANING OF OUR "HEART"?

WHO DOES JESUS HAVE IN MIND WHEN HE REFERS TO THE "PURE IN HEART"?

WHY DO YOU THINK IT IS THAT THE PURE IN HEART RECEIVE THE PROMISE: "FOR THEY WILL SEE GOD" (MATT. 5:8)?

MEDITATION AND APPLICATION

READ AND MEDITATE ON THE FOLLOWING VERSES. ASK THE FATHER TO REVEAL YOUR HEART TO YOU. PRAY THAT YOU MAY EXPERIENCE A RENEWAL OF YOUR HEART.

ABOVE ALL ELSE, GUARD YOUR HEART, FOR EVERYTHING YOU DO FLOWS FROM IT.

- PROVERBS 4:23

MAY THESE WORDS OF MY MOUTH AND THIS MEDITATION OF
MY HEART BE PLEASING IN YOUR SIGHT, LORD, MY ROCK AND
MY REDEEMER.

- PSALM 19:14

FOR WHERE YOUR TREASURE IS, THERE YOUR HEART WILL BE
ALSO.

- MATTHEW 6:21

LOVE THE LORD YOUR GOD WITH ALL YOUR HEART AND WITH
ALL YOUR SOUL AND WITH ALL YOUR MIND.

- MATTHEW 22:37

SINCE, THEN, YOU HAVE BEEN RAISED WITH CHRIST, SET YOUR
HEARTS ON THINGS ABOVE, WHERE CHRIST IS, SEATED AT THE
RIGHT HAND OF GOD.

- COLOSSIANS 3:1

the risk of authenticity

Yesterday, we looked at what Jesus meant when he blessed the pure in heart. The pure in heart are those whose purity begins in the very core of their being, a purity that drives all of their feelings, thoughts, and decisions.

The pure in heart don't live for others and don't care what others think of them; theirs is a hidden, inner purity.

We likely want this kind of inner purity. But there's a huge barrier that makes it difficult to achieve: *we are afraid to be our true selves.*

THE FEAR OF REJECTION

Kyle writes on page 90 in *The End of Me*:

> "We struggle with authenticity because we fear rejection. We want the world to see us at our very best, because then people are more likely to accept and possibly even admire us....

> Fear is the enemy of transparency. We don't like our flaws, and we don't expect anybody else to. So we work hard at putting up the most impressive front we can."

We have all experienced the pain of rejection.

You were cut from the team when you were in high school, but your best friends made varsity.

You didn't get into the college or grad school you desperately wanted to attend.

Your girlfriend or boyfriend dumped you to "date themselves," then ended up with someone else two weeks later.

Your boss told you your department was downsizing and your position was a casualty.

You discover a picture of your friends out having fun together on social media and you didn't get invited.

Unfortunately, rejection is a part of life. You can't possibly protect yourself from all rejection. To live is to be excluded, turned down, and pushed away.

So, what should we do—hide who we truly are, shut down our hearts and live without emotions, lock ourselves in the closet? There must be a better way.

THE RISK OF AUTHENTICITY

Authenticity is a risk. It exposes us to rejection.

We are afraid of being known because we have tried that before, with painful results.

But, as Kyle writes, "Getting to the end of me means I'm not worried about performing for others anymore" (91). There's a blessing in being ourselves.

The pure in heart are those who live from their core, whose feelings, thoughts, and decisions are driven by a secure center in Christ.

Later in his Sermon on the Mount, Jesus said,

> BE CAREFUL NOT TO PRACTICE YOUR RIGHTEOUSNESS IN FRONT OF OTHERS TO BE SEEN BY THEM. IF YOU DO, YOU WILL HAVE NO REWARD FROM YOUR FATHER IN HEAVEN.
>
> - MATTHEW 6:1

It's a risk to be authentic, to be pure in heart, to live only for God.

But there's a bigger risk: *In living to be seen by others, we risk losing God himself.* To put it another way: We have to become authentic to be accepted.

Instead, seek to please God first and let everything else be a distant second.

This is why Jesus's first Great Commandment is this: "Love the Lord your God with all your *heart* and with all your *soul* and with all your *mind*" (Matthew 22:37).

When you devote your heart, your soul, your mind—every fiber of your entire being—to the love of God, everything else falls into place.

Yes, you will still face occasional rejection. You may even be teased for seeking to love and live for God. But in the upside-down kingdom, this is true freedom.

When you come to the end of me and find yourself entirely in Christ, you discover God's blessing.

SCRIPTURE MEMORY

NOW WHEN JESUS SAW THE CROWDS, HE WENT UP ON A MOUNTAINSIDE AND SAT DOWN. AND HE BEGAN TO TEACH THEM. HE SAID: BLESSED ARE THE POOR IN SPIRIT, FOR THEIRS IS THE KINGDOM OF HEAVEN. BLESSED ARE THOSE WHO MOURN, FOR THEY WILL BE COMFORTED. BLESSED ARE THE MEEK, FOR THEY WILL INHERIT THE EARTH. BLESSED ARE THOSE WHO HUNGER AND THIRST FOR RIGHTEOUSNESS, FOR THEY WILL BE FILLED. BLESSED ARE THE MERCIFUL, FOR THEY WILL BE SHOWN MERCY. BLESSED ARE THE PURE IN HEART, FOR THEY WILL SEE GOD.

- MATTHEW 5:1-8

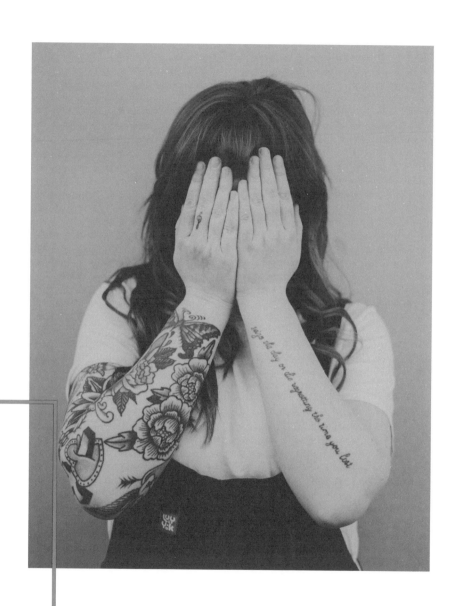

WHY ARE "THE PURE IN HEART" MARKED BY AUTHENTICITY?

WHY DOES JESUS USE SUCH STRONG LANGUAGE IN WARNING US ABOUT LIVING "TO BE SEEN BY OTHERS" (MATTHEW 6:1)?

HOW DOES OBEDIENCE TO THE GREAT COMMANDMENT (MATTHEW 22:37) GUARD US AGAINST LIVING FOR THE APPROVAL OF OTHERS?

QUESTIONS FOR REFLECTION

MEDITATION AND APPLICATION

READ MATTHEW 5:1-8 AGAIN SLOWLY AND REFLECT ON THE FOLLOWING QUESTIONS.

PICK ONE TIME IN YOUR LIFE WHEN YOU WERE REJECTED, LEFT OUT, OR PUSHED AWAY. WHAT HAPPENED? HOW DID IT FEEL AT THE TIME? HOW DO YOU THINK ABOUT IT WEEKS/MONTHS/YEARS LATER?

WHEN YOU THINK ABOUT YOUR CURRENT LIFE, WORK, AND RELATIONSHIPS, WHAT DO YOU FEAR LOSING THE MOST? WHY IS THIS PARTICULAR PERSON OR THING SO IMPORTANT TO YOU?

WHAT DOES IT LOOK LIKE FOR YOU TODAY TO MOVE FORWARD IN AUTHENTICITY, FEARING REJECTION, BUT VIEWING YOURSELF ENTIRELY THROUGH GOD'S EYES?

blessed are the little

Typically, we want to end up on top.

We want to stand on the highest platform to receive the gold medal. We want to be on top of the sales list, the grade chart, and the undiscussed ranking of who's who that people seem to have. Like a child on the playground, we want to be "king of the hill."

So Jesus's Beatitudes catch us off guard. It's not blessed to be on top, to be number one, to be the best and most accomplished.

The blessing is on the bottom.

BLESSINGS ON THE BOTTOM

Consider third of Jesus's beatitudes:

> BLESSED ARE THE MEEK, FOR
> THEY WILL INHERIT THE EARTH.
>
> - MATTHEW 5:5

Let's read it in another translation:

> GOD BLESSES
> THOSE WHO
> ARE HUMBLE,
> FOR THEY WILL
> INHERIT THE
> WHOLE EARTH
>
> - MATT. 5:5 NLT

The blessing of Christ is for the meek, the humble. But there's a translation I like even more—it comes from New Testament scholar Frederick Dale Bruner:

eople

> "**Blessings on *the little people*, because they will be granted the earth!**"

- FREDERICK DALE BRUNER

Why "little people"? As Bruner notes, "The little people are literally those who make no claims for themselves before God or before other people. They are perhaps best described as 'the powerless' or 'the oppressed.'"

The primary blessing of the third beatitude belongs to those in lowly places in life—the sick, the disabled, the poor, the oppressed, the marginalized. But there's also a blessing here for those who are little or lowly in heart—just like "the poor in spirit."

THEY WILL INHERIT THE EARTH

Jesus rocks us with this blessing on the little people of the world. Our world praises the big and bold, the dramatic and spectacular, the new and noteworthy.

According to our world: Blessed are the aggressive, and the world belongs to those who take it by force.

But Jesus flips it all upside down once again. Those who want to take over the whole world get...nothing. Those whom the world has walked on, climbed over, and raced past? They inherit the whole world.

Jesus put it like this in Luke 18:14.

> FOR ALL THOSE WHO EXALT THEMSELVES WILL BE HUMBLED,
> AND THOSE WHO HUMBLE THEMSELVES WILL BE EXALTED.

And this confirms God's heart throughout time:

> FOR THIS IS WHAT THE HIGH AND EXALTED ONE SAYS— HE
> WHO LIVES FOREVER, WHOSE NAME IS HOLY: 'I LIVE IN A HIGH
> AND HOLY PLACE, BUT ALSO WITH THE ONE WHO IS CONTRITE
> AND LOWLY IN SPIRIT, TO REVIVE THE SPIRIT OF THE LOWLY
> AND TO REVIVE THE HEART OF THE CONTRITE.'
>
> - ISAIAH 57:15

To put it simply:

> PRIDE BRINGS A PERSON LOW, BUT THE LOWLY IN SPIRIT GAIN
> HONOR.
>
> - PROVERBS 29:23

Now, where do we find a perfect example of this humility, meekness, and lowliness in human form?

KING OF HUMILITY

When we look at Jesus, once again, we find our beatitude embodied in his life and ministry. Jesus was the meekest, most humble, and "littlest" person ever to set foot on earth.

In Philippians, Paul urged the believers to become like Jesus. (This is a long text, but consider its power!)

JESUS CHRIST... WHO, BEING IN VERY NATURE GOD,
DID NOT CONSIDER EQUALITY WITH GOD SOMETHING
TO BE USED TO HIS OWN ADVANTAGE; RATHER, HE
MADE HIMSELF NOTHING BY TAKING THE VERY NATURE
OF A SERVANT, BEING MADE IN HUMAN LIKENESS.
AND BEING FOUND IN APPEARANCE AS A MAN, HE
HUMBLED HIMSELF BY BECOMING OBEDIENT TO
DEATH—EVEN DEATH ON A CROSS!

THEREFORE GOD EXALTED HIM TO THE HIGHEST PLACE
AND GAVE HIM THE NAME THAT IS ABOVE EVERY NAME,
THAT AT THE NAME OF JESUS EVERY KNEE SHOULD
BOW, IN HEAVEN AND ON EARTH AND UNDER THE
EARTH, AND EVERY TONGUE ACKNOWLEDGE THAT
JESUS CHRIST IS LORD, TO THE GLORY OF GOD THE
FATHER.

—PHILIPPIANS 2:6-11

If meekness, humility, and lowliness were blessing enough for Jesus—the eternal Son of God—then perhaps, just maybe, it's good enough for us.

SCRIPTURE MEMORY
REVIEW MATTHEW 5:1-9

CONTENT AND MEANING

HOW DOES THE THIRD BEATITUDE—BLESSED ARE THE MEEK—CONNECT TO THE TWO BEFORE IT? WHAT ABOUT THE ONES THAT FOLLOW IT?

IN WHAT SENSE IS JESUS'S BEATITUDE FOR THE SPIRITUALLY LOW (HUMBLE, MEEK)? HOW IS IT FOR THE PHYSICALLY LOW (POOR, MARGINALIZED, OPPRESSED)?

WHY IS IT SIGNIFICANT THAT THE PROMISE FOR THE MEEK IS THAT "THEY WILL INHERIT THE EARTH"?

MEDITATION AND APPLICATION

READ MATTHEW 5:1-9 AGAIN SLOWLY AND REFLECT ON THE FOLLOWING QUESTIONS.

WHAT FEARS DO YOU HAVE ABOUT EMBRACING A LIFE OF LOWLINESS, HUMILITY, AND MEEKNESS?

THINK OF SOMEONE YOU CONSIDER FITTING THE IMAGE THAT JESUS IS DESCRIBING. WHAT DO YOU APPRECIATE ABOUT HER/HIM? WOULD YOU SAY THAT THEY ARE WEAK, BORING, OR LESS IMPORTANT BECAUSE OF THEIR HUMILITY?

WHO IN YOUR LIFE IS IN A POSITION OF WORLDLY LOWLINESS (SICKNESS, DISABILITY, POVERTY), AND HOW CAN YOU SERVE AND LOVE HER/HIM TODAY?

the path to greatness

So far this week, we have explored two great themes from Jesus's teaching.

First, Jesus blesses *purity of heart*—a purity that begins in the very core of our being, a purity that drives all of our feelings, thoughts, and decisions. The truly Good Life means we stop worrying about others' opinions of ourselves. What matters is what's on the inside.

And second, Jesus blesses *lowliness of self*—when we seek to please him alone, we are free to accept a low, humble, meek position in life. Jesus honors the low and the little ones of the world.

Both of these truths fit our broader theme: In the kingdom of Christ, down is up, poverty is riches, and humility is greatness. When we reach the end of me, we find our true life.

Today, let's take another step on that path—the path to greatness.

A TALE OF TWO PRAYERS

One day, when Jesus was teaching in parables, he told a story of two men praying. It goes like this:

TO SOME WHO WERE CONFIDENT OF THEIR OWN RIGHTEOUSNESS AND LOOKED DOWN ON EVERYONE ELSE, JESUS TOLD THIS PARABLE: "TWO MEN WENT UP TO THE TEMPLE TO

PRAY, ONE A PHARISEE AND THE OTHER A TAX COLLECTOR."

- LUKE 18:9-10

Let's remember the context; the Pharisees were great men. They were among the religious leaders of their day, but they weren't mere scholars and scribes. The Pharisees were the popular, well-known, morally-right members of the religious hierarchy. They were a lot like pastors today—their job was to communicate the Scriptures to regular people and help women and men learn how to pray.

Of course, the Pharisees were also full of themselves. They were wise in their own eyes. They were proud of their "righteousness." They could list off their accomplishments. They had gone to the *right* schools, studied under the *right* scholars, and learned the *right* way to do things. Everything about them was *right*. All the time.

THE PHARISEE STOOD BY HIMSELF AND PRAYED: 'GOD, I THANK YOU THAT I AM NOT LIKE OTHER PEOPLE—ROBBERS, EVILDOERS, ADULTERERS—OR EVEN LIKE THIS TAX COLLECTOR. I FAST TWICE A WEEK AND GIVE A TENTH OF ALL I GET.'

- LUKE 18:11-12

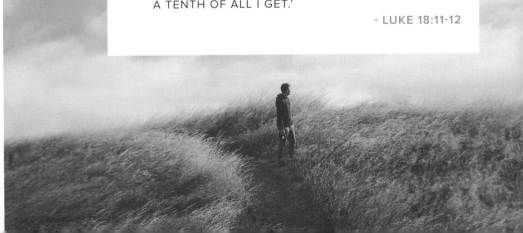

Tax collectors, on the other hand, were the wrong sort of people during this time. They were Israelites but worked for the Roman government, collecting taxes from their own people, but with Roman authority to take extra for themselves. They were debt collectors on commission—their salaries were provided by taking more than Rome needed, and as a result, they were frequently given to greed and improper techniques for tax collection.

They were the mobsters and drug dealers of their day—the ones you wanted to avoid, the ones who could end things for you if you crossed them the wrong way.

> BUT THE TAX COLLECTOR STOOD AT A DISTANCE. HE WOULD NOT EVEN LOOK UP TO HEAVEN, BUT BEAT HIS BREAST AND SAID, 'GOD, HAVE MERCY ON ME, A SINNER.'
>
> - LUKE 18:13

Notice the difference in prayer language. "If there's a pride index," Kyle writes, "it's the number of times you use first-person pronouns per hundred words." (79)

The Pharisee's prayer is self-centered and self-congratulating. It's all about himself. He even goes out of his way to condemn another person—"even like this tax collector"—in his prayer to God.

No one wants to be a Pharisee, but we have to admit we do this too. We might pray in special prayer language. We might reference our many previous prayers. We might even prayer-shame someone else: "I pray for self-control for my struggling friend here."

The tax collector doesn't do this. He prays in his own common language, praises God, owns his sin, and begs for mercy. It has been said that this simple seven-word prayer, often called the "Jesus Prayer" in monastic traditions, contains the entire message of Christianity:

God—praising the one true Creator and Lord of all for who he is

Have mercy on me—acknowledging that God alone gives mercy, and our salvation must come from outside of ourselves

A sinner—owning our sinfulness and turning to God for forgiveness and new life

Have you noticed that the tax collector fits the beatitudes?

He is *meek* and *poor in spirit*—his prayer is one of need, he begs God for mercy
He *mourns*—he beats his chest in agony over his brokenness
He *hungers for righteousness*—he doesn't claim his goodness but pleads for God's mercy
He is *pure in heart*—he wants only one thing, God's acceptance; it does not matter what the nearby Pharisee thinks of him

Once again, Jesus has brought us to the end of ourselves to receive the blessing. It's the tax collector who gets the blessing, not the religious superstar.

> "I TELL YOU THAT THIS MAN, RATHER THAN THE OTHER, WENT
> HOME JUSTIFIED BEFORE GOD. FOR ALL THOSE WHO EXALT
> THEMSELVES WILL BE HUMBLED, AND THOSE WHO HUMBLE
> THEMSELVES WILL BE EXALTED."
>
> - LUKE 18:14

It seems upside down. The whole kingdom does! But as Kyle puts it: "It seems like a reversal only because we have turned things in the wrong direction." (83)

The path to greatness is an indirect one. We must first move toward humility, meekness, and the end of me. In this lowliness and purity of heart, we discover true greatness—greatness in the kingdom.

THOSE
WHO
HUMBLE
THEMSELVES
WILL BE
EXALTED.

SCRIPTURE MEMORY

NOW WHEN JESUS SAW THE CROWDS, HE WENT UP ON A MOUNTAINSIDE AND SAT DOWN. AND HE BEGAN TO TEACH THEM. HE SAID: BLESSED ARE THE POOR IN SPIRIT, FOR THEIRS IS THE KINGDOM OF HEAVEN. BLESSED ARE THOSE WHO MOURN, FOR THEY WILL BE COMFORTED. BLESSED ARE THE MEEK, FOR THEY WILL INHERIT THE EARTH. BLESSED ARE THOSE WHO HUNGER AND THIRST FOR RIGHTEOUSNESS, FOR THEY WILL BE FILLED. BLESSED ARE THE MERCIFUL, FOR THEY WILL BE SHOWN MERCY. BLESSED ARE THE PURE IN HEART, FOR THEY WILL SEE GOD. BLESSED ARE THE PEACEMAKERS, FOR THEY WILL BE CALLED CHILDREN OF GOD.

- MATTHEW 5:1-9

CONTENT AND MEANING

HOW DOES THIS PARABLE DEMONSTRATE THE TWO THEMES—PURITY OF HEART AND LOWLINESS OF SELF? HOW DOES THE PHARISEE'S PRAYER ALSO DEMONSTRATE THE OPPOSITE OF THESE VIRTUES?

WHY DO YOU THINK JESUS CHOOSES A PHARISEE AND A TAX COLLECTOR FOR THIS PARABLE? WHAT IS THE SIGNIFICANCE OF EACH?

MEDITATION AND APPLICATION

READ LUKE 18:9-14 AGAIN SLOWLY AND REFLECT ON THE FOLLOWING QUESTIONS.

HOW DO YOU IDENTIFY WITH THE TAX COLLECTOR? HOW DO YOU SENSE YOUR OWN SIN, BROKENNESS, AND NEED OF GOD'S MERCY?

WHAT ARE SOME WAYS YOU IDENTIFY WITH THE PHARISEE?
WHEN HAVE YOU FELT YOURSELF LOOKING DOWN ON A
PERSON OR GROUP OF PEOPLE? WHEN YOU SENSE YOUR
"INNER PHARISEE" SPEAKING, WHAT IS BEING DEFENDED OR
PROMOTED WITHIN YOU?

REFLECT ON LUKE 18:14.

FOR ALL THOSE WHO EXALT THEMSELVES WILL BE

HUMBLED, AND THOSE WHO HUMBLE THEMSELVES

WILL BE EXALTED.

WHAT ARE FIVE OBSERVATIONS YOU HAVE ABOUT THIS
SINGLE VERSE?

authentic prayer

esus's Sermon on the Mount flips everything upside down.

But this one sermon was consistent with his entire life and ministry: He was turning the whole world upside down. Everything you thought you knew about God, religion, and everyday life—it all gets flipped by Christ.

Sickness and blindness were not supposed to exist in God's world, so Jesus healed the sick and gave sight to the blind. Demons were not supposed to roam freely, so Jesus freed the possessed and threw the demons into the pit of the sea. Death was an aspect of the curse, brought on by sin in Genesis 3, so Jesus reversed the curse and raised the dead.

In his teaching and his miracles, Jesus flips a broken world right-side up. Even if just for a moment, he pulls back the curtain on life the way it was meant to be—and the way it will be after his return, in the New Creation.

In Matthew 6, later in the Sermon on the Mount, we see a prime example of Jesus's redeeming work. Jesus taught his followers how to flip their own hearts right-side up. *He taught them how to pray.*

THE LORD'S PRAYER

You know these words well, but read them with fresh eyes, and consider the Beatitudes that precede this prayer just a chapter earlier.

AND WHEN YOU PRAY, DO NOT BE LIKE THE
HYPOCRITES, FOR THEY LOVE TO PRAY
STANDING IN THE SYNAGOGUES AND ON THE
STREET CORNERS TO BE SEEN BY OTHERS.
TRULY I TELL YOU, THEY HAVE RECEIVED THEIR
REWARD IN FULL. BUT WHEN YOU PRAY, GO
INTO YOUR ROOM, CLOSE THE DOOR AND PRAY
TO YOUR FATHER, WHO IS UNSEEN. THEN YOUR
FATHER, WHO SEES WHAT IS DONE IN SECRET,
WILL REWARD YOU. AND WHEN YOU PRAY, DO
NOT KEEP ON BABBLING LIKE PAGANS, FOR THEY
THINK THEY WILL BE HEARD BECAUSE OF THEIR
MANY WORDS. DO NOT BE LIKE THEM, FOR YOUR
FATHER KNOWS WHAT YOU NEED BEFORE YOU
ASK HIM. THIS, THEN, IS HOW YOU SHOULD PRAY:
'OUR FATHER IN HEAVEN,
HALLOWED BE YOUR NAME,
YOUR KINGDOM COME,
YOUR WILL BE DONE,
ON EARTH AS IT IS IN HEAVEN.
GIVE US TODAY OUR DAILY BREAD.
AND FORGIVE US OUR DEBTS,
AS WE ALSO HAVE FORGIVEN OUR DEBTORS.
AND LEAD US NOT INTO TEMPTATION,
BUT DELIVER US FROM THE EVIL ONE.'"

- MATTHEW 6:5-13

There is much we could say about this wonderful prayer. Let's just
focus on this one aspect today: *Jesus invites us to bring authentic
prayer before our heavenly Father.*

It would have been shocking for the disciples and other listeners to hear Jesus tell others to address God as Father. Although there were some examples of God's fatherly provision for Israel in the Old Testament, this is a brand-new and paradigm-shattering image. *The God of Israel is our Father?!*

PRAYING LIKE CHILDREN

Seeing God as our Father, this prayer begins to take shape. If God is our Father, then we are his daughters and sons. The apostle Paul writes, "So in Christ Jesus, you are all children of God through faith" (Galatians 3:26). The apostle John says, "See what great love the Father has lavished on us, that we should be called children of God! And that is what we are!" (1 John 3:1).

Jesus is inviting us to come to God the way a child comes to their father.

How do children approach their fathers? Do they use fancy language and carefully choose their words? Do they state their credentials before making their requests? Do they expect to be denied and rejected?

No way!

Think of how young children come to their father. Children approach their fathers with enthusiasm. They come exactly as they are and begin blurting out their requests, and no part of their mind thinks their request will be denied. And if their request is initially denied, what do they do? Ask again. And again. And again and again and again...

Kyle writes,
"Our ingrained mask-wearing keeps us from having the authentic, intimate relationship that Jesus wants to have with us... Getting to the end of me means I don't need to hide my flaws because I know his love is unconditional." (105)

When Jesus teaches his followers to pray, he invites them to approach God as his own beloved sons and daughters.

Nothing to prove, no fears, and no pretenses. You don't pray to be accepted. You have already been accepted in Christ. Prayer keeps us intimately connected to our Father!

SCRIPTURE MEMORY

NOW WHEN JESUS SAW THE CROWDS, HE WENT UP ON A MOUNTAINSIDE AND SAT DOWN. AND HE BEGAN TO TEACH THEM. HE SAID: BLESSED ARE THE POOR IN SPIRIT, FOR THEIRS IS THE KINGDOM OF HEAVEN. BLESSED ARE THOSE WHO MOURN, FOR THEY WILL BE COMFORTED. BLESSED ARE THE MEEK, FOR THEY WILL INHERIT THE EARTH. BLESSED ARE THOSE WHO HUNGER AND THIRST FOR RIGHTEOUSNESS, FOR THEY WILL BE FILLED. BLESSED ARE THE MERCIFUL, FOR THEY WILL BE SHOWN MERCY. BLESSED ARE THE PURE IN HEART, FOR THEY WILL SEE GOD. BLESSED ARE THE PEACEMAKERS, FOR THEY WILL BE CALLED CHILDREN OF GOD. BLESSED ARE THOSE WHO ARE PERSECUTED BECAUSE OF RIGHTEOUSNESS, FOR THEIRS IS THE KINGDOM OF HEAVEN.

- MATTHEW 5:1-10

CONTENT AND MEANING

HOW DOES JESUS TEACH HIS DISCIPLES NOT TO PRAY?
HOW DOES HE TEACH THEM TO PRAY INSTEAD?

WHAT DO YOU LEARN ABOUT JESUS AND THE CHRISTIAN
LIFE FROM THE CONTENT OF JESUS'S PRAYER?

WHAT PARALLELS DO YOU FIND BETWEEN THE BEATITUDES
AND THE LORD'S PRAYER?

MEDITATION AND APPLICATION

READ MATTHEW 6:5-13 AGAIN SLOWLY AND REFLECT ON THE FOLLOWING QUESTIONS.

HOW HAVE YOU BEEN TAUGHT TO PRAY THE LORD'S PRAYER? HOW DID YOU EXPERIENCE IT?

HOW DO YOU RESPOND TO THE INVITATION TO APPROACH GOD AS FATHER? WHAT WOULD IT LOOK LIKE TO COME AS A CHILD TO GOD?

OUR FATHER IN HEAVEN, HALLOWED BE YOUR NAME, YOUR KINGDOM COME, YOUR WILL BE DONE, ON EARTH AS IT IS IN HEAVEN. GIVE US TODAY OUR DAILY BREAD. AND FORGIVE US OUR DEBTS, AS WE ALSO HAVE FORGIVEN OUR DEBTORS. AND LEAD US NOT INTO TEMPTATION, BUT DELIVER US FROM THE EVIL ONE.

EXERCISE

WRITE OUT THE LORD'S PRAYER IN YOUR OWN WORDS, IN THE LANGUAGE YOU'D LIKE TO USE WITH YOUR HEAVENLY FATHER.

to see God's face

Jesus's blessings are for the poor in spirit, those who mourn, the little people, those who hunger and thirst for righteousness, and the pure in heart.

And the blessings themselves are rich indeed: Theirs is the kingdom; they will be comforted; they will inherit the earth; they will be satisfied. And my personal favorite—"They will see God."

> BLESSED ARE THE PURE IN HEART,
> FOR THEY WILL SEE GOD.
>
> - MATTHEW 6:8

TO SEE GOD'S FACE

What does Jesus mean by this promise? This is a question that New Testament scholars have debated for centuries.

The Psalms encourage us to "taste and see that the Lord is good" (Psalm 34:8), but this is even more direct. The apostle John says no one has seen God, but we experience him through the love of the Church (1 John 4:12). But this promise is clear: The pure in heart will see God.

Job believed that he would be restored from his sufferings: "In my flesh I will see God" (Job 19:26). John later wrote that "Anyone who does what is evil has not seen God" (3 John 1:11). So wait, did he see God?

As far as we can discern, Jesus's invitation means what it means: The pure in heart will see God. The Beatitudes extend to all who call on Jesus's name, and we can believe that through our oneness with Christ, *we too will see God.*

Although we can experience God here and now through his Word, in prayer, and through the fellowship with his daughters and sons in the Church, one day, our hope is this: We will see God face to face.

Like Moses in Exodus 33, we will one day speak to God "face to face, as one speaks to a friend" (Exodus 33:11).

For all eternity, our reward will not be mere comfort, security, or freedom from sin and brokenness. *Our reward will be God himself.* We will be with him as one is with a friend.

In this world, we must lay down ourselves. We must come to the end of ourselves. We must let God be enough in a world that says we need more.

But the reward of glory far outweighs the demand of obedience: *Blessed are the pure in heart, for they will see God!*

SCRIPTURE MEMORY
REVIEW MATTHEW 5:1-10

CONTENT AND MEANING

LOOKING JUST AT THE SECOND HALVES OF THE
BEATITUDES, WHAT STANDS OUT MOST? WHAT
QUESTIONS DO YOU HAVE?

WHAT DO YOU THINK OF THE SCRIPTURES' OCCASIONAL
REFERENCES TO SEEING GOD? HOW DO YOU READ AND
UNDERSTAND THESE PROMISES?

MEDITATION AND APPLICATION

READ MATTHEW 5:1-10 AGAIN SLOWLY AND REFLECT ON THE FOLLOWING QUESTIONS.

OF THE BEATITUDES THAT WE HAVE STUDIED IN THE PAST THREE WEEKS, WHICH ONE STANDS OUT TO YOU MOST PERSONALLY?

WHAT ENCOURAGES OR COMFORTS YOU SPECIFICALLY ABOUT THE PROMISE TO EXPERIENCE GOD PERSONALLY AND FOR ALL ETERNITY?

HOW COULD YOU USE THIS TRUTH TO MINISTER TO A BELIEVING FRIEND, COWORKER, OR FAMILY MEMBER? HOW MIGHT THIS ENCOURAGE SOMEONE STRUGGLING AND FEELING DISTANT FROM THE LORD?

REFLECTION & REVIEW

O n the seventh day of each week, we're going to pause to review and reflect on the past week.

If you are behind a day or two, use this day to catch up.

If you are caught up, use this day to review the previous six days' notes—especially all the Scripture references and stories. Use these seventh days to review your Scripture memory verses as well.

SCRIPTURE MEMORY

REVIEW MATTHEW 5:1-10

NOW WHEN JESUS SAW THE CROWDS, HE WENT UP ON A MOUNTAINSIDE AND SAT DOWN. AND HE BEGAN TO TEACH THEM. HE SAID: BLESSED ARE THE POOR IN SPIRIT, FOR THEIRS IS THE KINGDOM OF HEAVEN. BLESSED ARE THOSE WHO MOURN, FOR THEY WILL BE COMFORTED. BLESSED ARE THE MEEK, FOR THEY WILL INHERIT THE EARTH. BLESSED ARE THOSE WHO HUNGER AND THIRST FOR RIGHTEOUSNESS, FOR THEY WILL BE FILLED. BLESSED ARE THE MERCIFUL, FOR THEY WILL BE SHOWN MERCY. BLESSED ARE THE PURE IN HEART, FOR THEY WILL SEE GOD. BLESSED ARE THE PEACEMAKERS, FOR THEY WILL BE CALLED CHILDREN OF GOD. BLESSED ARE THOSE WHO ARE PERSECUTED BECAUSE OF RIGHTEOUSNESS, FOR THEIRS IS THE KINGDOM OF HEAVEN.

QUESTIONS FOR REFLECTION

BASED ON YOUR WEEK'S READING AND
REFLECTION, ANSWER THE FOLLOWING
QUESTIONS.

WHAT WAS THE MOST SIGNIFICANT THING I
LEARNED ABOUT JESUS AND THE CHRISTIAN
LIFE THIS WEEK?

WHAT WAS THE MOST SIGNIFICANT THING
I LEARNED ABOUT POVERTY OF SPIRIT,
BROKENNESS, AND WHOLENESS THIS WEEK?

WHAT WAS THE MOST SIGNIFICANT THING I LEARNED ABOUT MYSELF THIS WEEK?

WHAT WOULD MY LIFE LOOK LIKE IF I FULLY BELIEVED AND LIVED EVERYTHING I READ AND WROTE THIS WEEK?

EMPTY TO BE FILLED

*Rejoice and be glad, because
great is your reward in heaven.*

Matthew 5:12

FOUR

where strength begins

When Jesus sat down on that green mountainside in Galilee, everything was about to change.

On the surface, everything sounds upside down. Jesus says, blessed are the down and out, the mourners, those who lack, the little people, the pure and merciful, and the unpopular.

We expect an invitation to the Good Life to include promises of comfort, stability, acceptance, and status.

But when we press in, we discover Jesus's insight and wisdom—a wisdom that is not of this world. He knows that comfort is momentary, stability is unguaranteed, acceptance is fleeting, and status is temporary. Nothing good in this world lasts long. What we need, then, is not of this world at all.

For Jesus, what's eternal comes through what's difficult:

Brokenness is the way to wholeness.
Mourning is the way to happiness.
Authenticity is the way to acceptance.

And this week, we'll discover one final and critical element of Jesus's teaching: *Emptiness is the way to fullness.*

According to Jesus, blessings begin in brokenness, mourning, humility, and authenticity. So where does strength begin?

THE PARADOX OF STRENGTH

We all want to be strong. We want to be chosen for the team, equipped for the task, and empowered for the battle.

But—as you may have suspected by now—strength, power, and fullness don't come by pursuing them directly, not in Jesus's upside-down kingdom.

We are full in our emptiness.
We are empowered in our helplessness.
We are chosen in our disqualification.
We are strongest in our weakness.

Why? Because Jesus loves to fill what's empty, empower what's powerless, choose what's unchosen, and strengthen what's weak.

ETERNAL TREASURE IN CLAY JARS

A great picture of this comes from the apostle Paul. When Paul first met Jesus, he wasn't even Paul. His name was Saul, and he was a Pharisee and a fierce opponent of Christianity. But after meeting Jesus, everything changed. His passion and intellect were emptied—he lost all of his credibility as a Jewish scholar and leader. Yet in his emptiness, he was filled; in his rejection, he found ultimate acceptance.

So it should come as no surprise that when his credibility was challenged, his response was Christlike.

In 2 Corinthians 4, Paul writes that we have the beauty of the Gospel—the Good News that God chooses what's weak and broken in Christ—in clay jars. The most powerful, most beautiful of all things dwells in the humblest of containers. Why?

WE HAVE THIS TREASURE IN JARS OF CLAY TO SHOW THAT
THIS ALL-SURPASSING POWER IS FROM GOD AND NOT FROM
US

- 2 CORINTHIANS 4:7

If our power has been given by man, it can quickly be taken. But power from God is incomparable, unmatched, and eternal.

When we are weak, God has a humble vessel, a clay jar from which he can display the beauty of his work through Christ.

Where does strength begin? It begins with our weakness. When we are weak, God's eternal power is on full display.

SCRIPTURE MEMORY

NOW WHEN JESUS SAW THE CROWDS, HE WENT UP ON A MOUNTAINSIDE AND SAT DOWN. AND HE BEGAN TO TEACH THEM. HE SAID: BLESSED ARE THE POOR IN SPIRIT, FOR THEIRS IS THE KINGDOM OF HEAVEN. BLESSED ARE THOSE WHO MOURN, FOR THEY WILL BE COMFORTED. BLESSED ARE THE MEEK, FOR THEY WILL INHERIT THE EARTH. BLESSED ARE THOSE WHO HUNGER AND THIRST FOR RIGHTEOUSNESS, FOR THEY WILL BE FILLED. BLESSED ARE THE MERCIFUL, FOR THEY WILL BE SHOWN MERCY. BLESSED ARE THE PURE IN HEART, FOR THEY WILL SEE GOD. BLESSED ARE THE PEACEMAKERS, FOR THEY WILL BE CALLED CHILDREN OF GOD. BLESSED ARE THOSE WHO ARE PERSECUTED BECAUSE OF RIGHTEOUSNESS, FOR THEIRS IS THE KINGDOM OF HEAVEN. BLESSED ARE YOU WHEN PEOPLE INSULT YOU, PERSECUTE YOU AND FALSELY SAY ALL KINDS OF EVIL AGAINST YOU BECAUSE OF ME.

- MATTHEW 5:1-11

CONTENT AND MEANING

WHERE IN OUR WORLD—TV, MOVIES, SPORTS, POLITICS, ETC.—
DO YOU SEE PUBLIC DISPLAYS OF STRENGTH AND POWER?

WHY ARE WE DRAWN TO THE STRONG AND POWERFUL?

READ 2 CORINTHIANS 4:7-18. HOW DOES PAUL'S TEACHING
AFFIRM JESUS'S BEATITUDES? WHAT PARALLELS DO YOU SEE
AND WHAT DIFFERENT EMPHASES DO YOU FIND?

HOW DOES PAUL'S LIFE DEMONSTRATE THE THEME OF JESUS'S
TEACHING IN THE BEATITUDES?

MEDITATION AND APPLICATION

READ MATTHEW 5:1-11 AGAIN SLOWLY AND REFLECT ON THE FOLLOWING QUESTIONS.

HOW DO YOU FEEL ABOUT BEING REFERRED TO AS A CLAY JAR—A SIMPLE, UNSPECTACULAR VESSEL FOR GOD'S ALL-SURPASSING GLORY?

HOW HAVE YOU EXPERIENCED PAUL'S TESTIMONY OF BEING "HARD PRESSED ON EVERY SIDE, BUT NOT CRUSHED" IN 2 CORINTHIANS 4:8-9?

HOW HAVE YOU EXPERIENCED GOD'S POWER AND COMFORT IN TIMES OF NEED AND PAIN?

IS THERE ANYONE IN YOUR LIFE NOW WHO COULD BE ENCOURAGED AND COMFORTED BY THIS MESSAGE OF GOD'S POWER FOR THE WEAK AND EMPTY?

filling what's empty

This week, we're looking at how Jesus fills what's empty, strengthens what's weak, and empowers what's helpless.

As Kyle Idleman writes in *The End of Me*: "God is a filler of empty spaces, and Jesus was a living picture of what that means." (114)

This picture—God filling what's empty—is entirely countercultural. It challenges the constant advertising of our day and threatens to bring down entire industries of excessive-want.

THE CAVITY OF THE SOUL

We always want just a little bit more. Kyle describes the experience of flipping through the SkyMall magazine tucked in the back of airplane seats. Gadgets and devices and thingamajigs for just about everything—whether you need them or not. The entire catalog features things we didn't know existed but now we must have!

My favorite hobby is cycling. I have a road bicycle and love to go on long rides. But I find myself always wanting the latest upgrade or newest feature. There's a joke in the cycling world that asks, "How many bikes do you need?" And the correct response is "The number of bikes I have, plus one." Just a little bit more.

Mother Teresa said this:

> **"The spiritual poverty of the Western world is much greater than the physical poverty of our people in Calcutta. You in the West have millions of people who suffer such terrible loneliness and emptiness…. These people are not hungry in the physical sense, but they are in another way. They know they need something more than money, yet they don't know what it is. What they are missing really is a living relationship with God." (*The End of Me* 123)**

MOTHER TERESA

It's a sobering thought. Our many attempts to fill ourselves through possessions and experiences have left us emptier than ever. By pursuing fullness directly, we've found only emptiness.

As Kyle puts it,

"We're trying to fill the cavity of the soul with things that won't fit." (123)

If the pursuit of fullness has left us empty, then what do we do? Perhaps the way to fullness is instead through emptiness.

CONTENTMENT WITH GODLINESS

In 1 Timothy, Paul writes a warning to his young friend about the disease of "just a little bit more".

> BUT GODLINESS WITH CONTENTMENT IS GREAT GAIN. FOR WE BROUGHT NOTHING INTO THE WORLD, AND WE CAN TAKE NOTHING OUT OF IT. BUT IF WE HAVE FOOD AND CLOTHING, WE WILL BE CONTENT WITH THAT. THOSE WHO WANT TO GET RICH FALL INTO TEMPTATION AND A TRAP AND INTO MANY FOOLISH AND HARMFUL DESIRES THAT PLUNGE PEOPLE INTO RUIN AND DESTRUCTION. FOR THE LOVE OF MONEY IS A ROOT OF ALL KINDS OF EVIL. SOME PEOPLE, EAGER FOR MONEY, HAVE WANDERED FROM THE FAITH AND PIERCED THEMSELVES WITH MANY GRIEFS.

- 1 TIMOTHY 6:6-10

This seems like a hard truth at first: We brought nothing into this world, and we can take nothing from it. But it's actually quite liberating. God promises to provide for us (Matthew 6:25-34). What really matters in this world is not what's seen but what's unseen—because what's invisible is eternal (2 Corinthians 4:18).

So, we can give up the pursuit of "just a little bit more" and let God be God—a filler of empty spaces.

If there's a cavity in your soul, no amount of money, no new gadget or trinket, no bit of status or accomplishment, and no position or authority will be able to fill that void.

Only God can fill what's empty.

NOW WHEN JESUS SAW THE CROWDS, HE WENT UP ON A MOUNTAINSIDE AND SAT DOWN. AND HE BEGAN TO TEACH THEM. HE SAID: BLESSED ARE THE POOR IN SPIRIT, FOR THEIRS IS THE KINGDOM OF HEAVEN. BLESSED ARE THOSE WHO MOURN, FOR THEY WILL BE COMFORTED. BLESSED ARE THE MEEK, FOR THEY WILL INHERIT THE EARTH. BLESSED ARE THOSE WHO HUNGER AND THIRST FOR RIGHTEOUSNESS, FOR THEY WILL BE FILLED. BLESSED ARE THE MERCIFUL, FOR THEY WILL BE SHOWN MERCY. BLESSED ARE THE PURE IN HEART, FOR THEY WILL SEE GOD. BLESSED ARE THE PEACEMAKERS, FOR THEY WILL BE CALLED CHILDREN OF GOD. BLESSED ARE THOSE WHO ARE PERSECUTED BECAUSE OF RIGHTEOUSNESS, FOR THEIRS IS THE KINGDOM OF HEAVEN. BLESSED ARE YOU WHEN PEOPLE INSULT YOU, PERSECUTE YOU AND FALSELY SAY ALL KINDS OF EVIL AGAINST YOU BECAUSE OF ME.

- MATTHEW 5:1-11

CONTENT AND MEANING

READ PHILIPPIANS 2:5-11 AGAIN. IN WHAT SENSE DID JESUS "MAKE HIMSELF NOTHING" OR "EMPTY HIMSELF" (V. 7)?

WHAT DID JESUS GIVE UP? WHAT DID HE NOT LOSE?

WHAT PARALLELS DO YOU SEE BETWEEN MATTHEW 5:1-12 AND PHILIPPIANS 2:5-11? HOW DOES JESUS EMBODY MATTHEW 5:10 OF HIS OWN TEACHING, "BLESSED ARE THOSE WHO ARE PERSECUTED BECAUSE OF RIGHTEOUSNESS, FOR THEIRS IS THE KINGDOM OF HEAVEN"?

MEDITATION AND APPLICATION

WHERE DO YOU FIND YOURSELF WANTING "JUST A LITTLE BIT MORE"?

HOW DOES THE MOTHER TERESA QUOTE CHALLENGE, CONVICT, OR INSPIRE YOU?

CONSIDER PAUL'S TEACHING IN 1 TIMOTHY 6:6-10. HOW DO YOU SENSE GOD INVITING YOU INTO A LIFE OF "GODLINESS WITH CONTENTMENT"?

DAY 24

a feast for the least

God loves to fill what's empty and empower what's weak. The path to fullness, then, is through emptiness, and the path to strength is through weakness. Jesus once told a parable with shocking implications to demonstrate this point.

THE PARABLE OF THE GREAT BANQUET

As the parable goes (Luke 14:16-24), a wealthy man prepared a feast fit for kings and nobles. But upon inviting his friends, each came up with an excuse not to attend.

One said, "I have just bought a field, and I must go and see it." He was more interested in personal gain than a feast with friends and neighbors.

Another said, "I have just bought five yokes of oxen, and I'm on my way to try them out." He was too concerned with his work and responsibility. He was too busy.

And one other said, "I just got married, so I can't come." He was satisfied with his new domestic cocoon and didn't want his comfort disturbed.

Possessions. Busyness. Comfort. These are the things standing between the men and the most wonderful feast of their lives.

In the Scriptures, feasts are not just meals. Kyle writes, "a banquet... is often a metaphor for how God addresses the deepest needs of his people.... The symbolism is natural: the Master feeding his people, giving them not only food but *very fine food*—a simple and powerful image of God." (118)

BRING IN THE POOR AND THE LAME

As the parable continues, the banquet master refuses to have his feast go to waste. He tells his servant, "Go out quickly into the streets and alleys and bring in the poor, the crippled, the blind, and the lame" (v21). And when there were still seats left: "Go out to the roads and the country lanes and compel them to come in, so that my house will be full" (v23).

So the ones who were too preoccupied—with their stuff, their activities, their romantic lives—missed out on the feast. And the parable has this shocking meaning: *If you're too busy, too full of yourself to need God, you will miss the Great Banquet.*

For the Jews, it was a preview of things to come: Their people would not receive Christ, so the Gospel would spread to the Gentiles (see Acts 8-15).

For us today, the great Banquet Master has sent out his invitation. The feast is on the table. But the questions remain:

Is there anything more important to us than responding to God's invitation?
What would be your most likely reason for walking away?
What takes up the space in your life that is meant for God?

As Kyle writes, "The measure of filling we receive is in direct proportion to the level of our emptiness. Don't settle for the full life—go after the filled life." (130)

SCRIPTURE MEMORY

NOW WHEN JESUS SAW THE CROWDS, HE WENT UP ON A MOUNTAINSIDE AND SAT DOWN. AND HE BEGAN TO TEACH THEM. HE SAID: BLESSED ARE THE POOR IN SPIRIT, FOR THEIRS IS THE KINGDOM OF HEAVEN. BLESSED ARE THOSE WHO MOURN, FOR THEY WILL BE COMFORTED. BLESSED ARE THE MEEK, FOR THEY WILL INHERIT THE EARTH. BLESSED ARE THOSE WHO HUNGER AND THIRST FOR RIGHTEOUSNESS, FOR THEY WILL BE FILLED. BLESSED ARE THE MERCIFUL, FOR THEY WILL BE SHOWN MERCY. BLESSED ARE THE PURE IN HEART, FOR THEY WILL SEE GOD. BLESSED ARE THE PEACEMAKERS, FOR THEY WILL BE CALLED CHILDREN OF GOD. BLESSED ARE THOSE WHO ARE PERSECUTED BECAUSE OF RIGHTEOUSNESS, FOR THEIRS IS THE KINGDOM OF HEAVEN. BLESSED ARE YOU WHEN PEOPLE INSULT YOU, PERSECUTE YOU AND FALSELY SAY ALL KINDS OF EVIL AGAINST YOU BECAUSE OF ME. REJOICE AND BE GLAD, BECAUSE GREAT IS YOUR REWARD IN HEAVEN, FOR IN THE SAME WAY THEY PERSECUTED THE PROPHETS WHO WERE BEFORE YOU.   - MATTHEW 5:1-12

CONTENT AND MEANING

READ LUKE 14:16-24. HOW DO YOU SEE THIS PARABLE
ILLUSTRATE THE TRUTHS OF MATTHEW 5:1-12?

PUT THE THREE EXCUSES OF LUKE 14:18-20 INTO YOUR OWN
WORDS. WHY DO THESE INVITEES RESIST? WHAT OTHER
COMMON EXCUSES KEEP PEOPLE FROM GOD'S FEAST?

QUESTIONS FOR REFLECTION

MEDITATION AND APPLICATION

READ MATTHEW 5:1-12 AGAIN SLOWLY AND REFLECT ON THE FOLLOWING QUESTIONS.

HOW DOES THIS PARABLE CHALLENGE, CONVICT, OR ENCOURAGE YOU?

WAS THERE A TIME IN YOUR LIFE WHERE SOMETHING WAS MORE IMPORTANT TO YOU THAN A HEART RESPONSIVE TO GOD?

WHAT HAS GOD SET ON YOUR HEART THAT MIGHT BE IN THE PLACE OF HIS PRESENCE? WHAT IS TAKING UP SPACE IN YOUR HEART MEANT FOR GOD?

helpless to be empowered

When we are most empty, we are in the best place to be filled. When we are weakest, we can become vessels for God's glory. When we are most helpless, we are best positioned to be empowered.

In John 5:1-15, we see Jesus embodying the principles taught throughout the Beatitudes.

A POOLSIDE HEALING

In Jerusalem, there was a famous pool called Bethesda. Legend had it that angels would come down and touch the waters, and who-ever was the first person into the water afterward would be healed. As a result, the pool was a home-away-from-home for the blind, the lame, and the paralyzed.

One day, as Jesus was passing by, he focused his attention on one particular man. This man had

been paralyzed for 38 years, and he had been waiting by the pool in hopes of healing for decades. Jesus's first question to the man is startling: "Do you want to get well?"

Now, why would Jesus ask that?

Of course, this man wanted to get well. He was paralyzed; he had lived most of his life in pain and stillness; he was at the one place where he believed healing could be found. But still, Jesus asked the question.

Jesus often does this. Outside Jericho, Bartimaeus and another blind man call out to Jesus, and he responds, "What do you want me to do for you?" (Matthew 20:29-34; Mark 10:46-52; Luke 18:35-43). When James and John come to him with a request, he asks "What do you want me to do for you?" (Mark 10:36).

He asks the person he plans to heal to vocalize precisely what it is they want and need. He wants to heal us, but he wants us to bring our need for healing to him. It's not a game, but he knows we have to recognize our need before he can meet it.

"Who wouldn't want help?" Kyle writes, "Someone in denial of reality." (142)

Many of us don't want healing because we fear change. We're afraid of losing control. We're unwilling to face the reality of our position. We are totally helpless, and we need help.

HELP FOR THE HELPLESS

Returning to our story, Jesus looks the paralyzed man in the eyes and asks his question. The man responds that there's no one to help him into the waters. He does want help. He is in need. He embraces his reality but doesn't know where to find help.

Fortunately, he is looking into the eyes of the Savior of the world.

As the text says,

> THEN JESUS SAID TO HIM, 'GET UP! PICK UP YOUR MAT AND WALK.' AT ONCE, THE MAN WAS CURED; HE PICKED UP HIS MAT AND WALKED.
>
> - JOHN 5:8-9

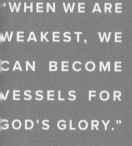

'WHEN WE ARE WEAKEST, WE CAN BECOME VESSELS FOR GOD'S GLORY."

This is the way of God: When we are in need, he provides. When we are most helpless, he gives his power. When we reach the end of ourselves, Jesus can finally get started.

As the pastor D.L. Moody once put it:

> **"God sends no one away empty except those who are full of themselves."**
>
> - D.L. MOODY

NOW WHEN JESUS SAW THE CROWDS, HE WENT UP ON A MOUNTAINSIDE AND SAT DOWN. AND HE BEGAN TO TEACH THEM. HE SAID: BLESSED ARE THE POOR IN SPIRIT, FOR THEIRS IS THE KINGDOM OF HEAVEN. BLESSED ARE THOSE WHO MOURN, FOR THEY WILL BE COMFORTED. BLESSED ARE THE MEEK, FOR THEY WILL INHERIT THE EARTH. BLESSED ARE THOSE WHO HUNGER AND THIRST FOR RIGHTEOUSNESS, FOR THEY WILL BE FILLED. BLESSED ARE THE MERCIFUL, FOR THEY WILL BE SHOWN MERCY. BLESSED ARE THE PURE IN HEART, FOR THEY WILL SEE GOD. BLESSED ARE THE MERCIFUL, FOR THEY WILL BE SHOWN MERCY. BLESSED ARE THE PURE IN HEART, FOR THEY WILL SEE GOD. BLESSED ARE THE PEACEMAKERS, FOR THEY WILL BE CALLED CHILDREN OF GOD. BLESSED ARE THOSE WHO ARE PERSECUTED BECAUSE OF RIGHTEOUSNESS, FOR THEIRS IS THE KINGDOM OF HEAVEN. BLESSED ARE YOU WHEN PEOPLE INSULT YOU, PERSECUTE YOU AND FALSELY SAY ALL KINDS OF EVIL AGAINST YOU BECAUSE OF ME. REJOICE AND BE GLAD, BECAUSE GREAT IS YOUR REWARD IN HEAVEN, FOR IN THE SAME WAY THEY PERSECUTED THE PROPHETS WHO WERE BEFORE YOU.

- MATTHEW 5:1-12

CONTENT AND MEANING

READ JOHN 5:1-15. HOW DOES THIS ENCOUNTER WITH JESUS ILLUSTRATE HIS TEACHING IN MATTHEW 5:1-12? WHICH BEATITUDE STANDS OUT IN CONNECTION WITH THIS STORY?

WHY WOULD SOMEONE IN NEED OF HEALING NOT WANT IT? WHAT KEEPS PEOPLE FROM ASKING FOR HELP?

QUESTIONS FOR REFLECTION

MEDITATION AND APPLICATION

READ MATTHEW 5:1-12 AGAIN SLOWLY AND REFLECT ON THE FOLLOWING QUESTIONS.

HOW DO YOU RESONATE WITH THIS STORY? WHERE IN YOUR LIFE ARE YOU IN NEED? WHY MIGHT YOU RESIST BRINGING THAT NEED BEFORE CHRIST?

HOW ARE YOU ENCOURAGED BY THIS STORY AND BY JESUS'S FIRST BEATITUDE: "BLESSED ARE THE POOR IN SPIRIT, FOR THEIRS IS THE KINGDOM OF HEAVEN"? WHAT DOES IT LOOK LIKE FOR YOU TO EMBRACE YOUR NEED OF GOD TODAY?

emptied to be full

J esus knows that comfort is momentary, stability is unguaranteed, acceptance is fleeting, and status is temporary. Nothing good in this world lasts long. What we need, then, is not of this world at all.

For Jesus, what's eternal comes through what's difficult: Brokenness is the way to wholeness. Mourning is the way to happiness. Authenticity is the way to acceptance.

And emptiness is the way to fullness.

MADE HIMSELF NOTHING

Jesus is the perfect demonstration of being empty to be filled. In Philippians 2:1-11, Paul describes the nature of Jesus's mission on earth—it was possibly an ancient creed of the early church. (We looked at this briefly on Day 17, but let's return for a deeper look.)

> JESUS CHRIST... WHO, BEING IN VERY NATURE GOD, DID NOT
> CONSIDER EQUALITY WITH GOD SOMETHING TO BE USED
> TO HIS OWN ADVANTAGE;
> RATHER, HE MADE HIMSELF NOTHING BY TAKING THE VERY
> NATURE OF A SERVANT,
> BEING MADE IN HUMAN LIKENESS.

AND BEING FOUND IN APPEARANCE AS A MAN,

HE HUMBLED HIMSELF

BY BECOMING OBEDIENT TO DEATH—

EVEN DEATH ON A CROSS!

THEREFORE GOD EXALTED HIM TO THE HIGHEST PLACE

AND GAVE HIM THE NAME THAT IS ABOVE EVERY NAME,

THAT AT THE NAME OF JESUS EVERY KNEE SHOULD

BOW, IN HEAVEN AND ON EARTH AND UNDER THE

EARTH, AND EVERY TONGUE ACKNOWLEDGE THAT

JESUS CHRIST IS LORD, TO THE GLORY OF GOD THE

FATHER.

- PHILIPPIANS 2:6-11

Jesus Christ is the eternal Son of God. He wasn't created. Instead, he is the co-Creator of the universe. He has lived in eternal glory and love with the Father and the Holy Spirit in the fellowship of the Trinity. As Hebrews says, Christ is "the radiance of God's glory and the exact representation of his being, sustaining all things by his powerful word" (Hebrews 1:3).

Even Jesus Christ, the eternal Son of God, "emptied himself" (Philippians 2:7 ESV). He didn't give up his lordship, but "he did not consider equality with God something to be used for his own advantage" (Philippians 2:6). He made himself low, vulnerable, and weak by becoming human so that he might save us. He was born into poverty and lived his first few years as a refugee in a foreign land. He was raised in a normal, lower-class home and embraced every aspect of ordinary, simple human life.

And as if that wasn't enough, Jesus's humility led him all the way to Calvary. He was wrongly accused, carried his own cross, suffered without relief, was abandoned in his time of need, and even then, remained faithful to his Father and his calling.

Jesus emptied himself not just so he could be filled—but so that every one of us might be offered true and eternal fullness.

Jesus's ultimate sacrifice led to his eternal glorification. "God exalted him to the highest place and gave him the name that is above every name" (Philippians 2:9).

His life, death, and resurrection secured our salvation. And his way also establishes a pattern for us. It's better to serve than to be served, better to give than to receive, and better to be emptied than filled—so that ultimate fullness can be given from God.

SCRIPTURE MEMORY
REVIEW MATTHEW 5:1-12

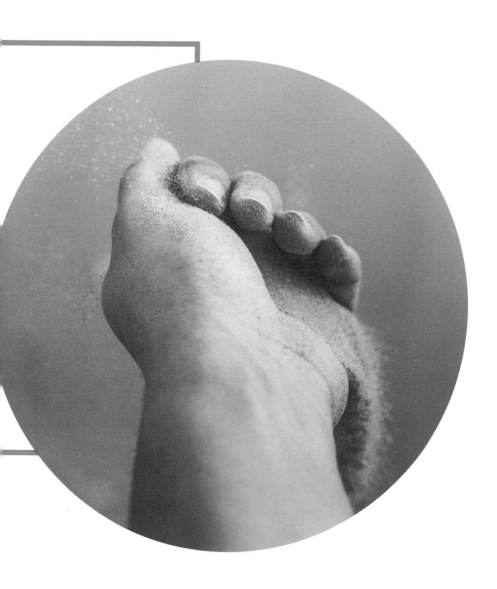

"JESUS IS THE PERFECT DEMONSTRATION
OF BEING EMPTIED TO BE FILLED."

CONTENT AND MEANING

READ PHILIPPIANS 2:5-11 AGAIN. WHAT IS THE PRIMARY MEANING OF THIS TEXT? HOW DOES IT RELATE TO OR DEMONSTRATE JESUS'S TEACHING IN MATTHEW 5:1-12?

READ PHILIPPIANS 2:1-4. HOW DOES PAUL URGE THE BELIEVERS TO UNITY AND CHRISTLIKENESS—USING JESUS'S HUMILITY AS AN EXAMPLE? HOW DO VERSES 1-4 CHANGE THE WAY YOU READ VERSES 5-11?

MEDITATION AND APPLICATION

**READ MATTHEW 5:1-12 AGAIN SLOWLY AND REFLECT ON
THE FOLLOWING QUESTIONS.**

WHERE DO YOU SENSE GOD CALLING YOU TO EMBODY THE
PATTERN OF CHRIST—TO NOT TAKE ADVANTAGE OF A GIFT
OR RESOURCE, BUT INSTEAD TO LEVERAGE IT FOR THE
GOOD OF OTHERS?

THINK OF THE PROMISE BEHIND JESUS'S FINAL BEATITUDE:
"REJOICE AND BE GLAD, BECAUSE GREAT IS YOUR REWARD
IN HEAVEN, FOR IN THE SAME WAY THEY PERSECUTED
THE PROPHETS WHO WERE BEFORE YOU." HOW ARE YOU
INSPIRED BY THIS PROMISE?

the end of you

n Jesus's Beatitudes, he is flipping an upside-down world right-side up. You can't find what you're looking for—happiness, peace, meaning, acceptance, and legacy—by pursuing it directly.

In other words, you've been lied to your whole life.

THE PATH BEFORE US

"There is a path before each person that seems right," Proverbs 14:12 says, "but it ends in death." On the other hand, there's a path that seems wrong to us, but in the end, it leads to life.

As Jesus said to his disciples,

> "WHOEVER WANTS TO BE MY DISCIPLE MUST DENY THEMSELVES AND TAKE UP THEIR CROSS AND FOLLOW ME. FOR WHOEVER WANTS TO SAVE THEIR LIFE WILL LOSE IT, BUT WHOEVER LOSES THEIR LIFE FOR ME WILL FIND IT."
>
> - MATTHEW 16:24-25

The way we expect to lead to life is a dead end. But there's another way, a better path, and it offers a new beginning.

Kyle writes, "Coming to the end of me also means allowing Jesus to put an end to the guilt and shame of the past. He deletes your permanent record and offers you a new beginning with a new purpose." (165)

SCRIP

REVIEW

What is standing in the way of your new beginning and new purpose? True blessedness isn't found in looking within ourselves or developing self-esteem. The Good Life isn't found by focusing on me at all. Instead, blessedness is found in less of me and more of Christ.

Brokenness is the way to wholeness. Mourning is the way to happiness. Authenticity is the way to acceptance. And emptiness is the way to fullness.

When you come to the end of me, you are free to live as Christ intended—free to be truly blessed.

THE END OF ME—EVERY DAY

This is not a once-in-a-lifetime challenge. It is a daily one.

"Each day is a new narrow gate. The problem with dying to myself is that it's so daily. I have to make the choice over and over again. I can live for myself or I can live for Christ, which means picking up my cross." (Idleman 204)

If we will open our eyes to it, God is working all around us, always present, always inviting us out of ourselves and into his blessing. Denying ourselves, taking the narrow path, and loving others isn't an occasional option. It's a daily choice, a way of life that changes everything.

The end of me requires not just a death, but a daily dying. When we come to the end of ourselves, we discover we have reached the place we've been seeking all along.

At the end of me, real life begins.

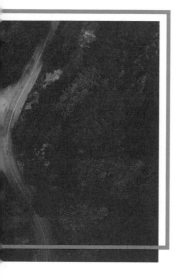

RE MEMORY

ATTHEW 5:1-12

QUESTIONS FOR REFLECTION

CONTENT AND MEANING

WHAT DOES JESUS MEAN WHEN HE CALLS US TO TAKE UP OUR CROSSES AND DIE TO OURSELVES (MATTHEW 16:24-25)?

HOW DOES JESUS'S TEACHING IN MATTHEW 16:24-25 RELATE TO HIS BEATITUDES? HOW DO YOU SEE THE PARADOXICAL TEACHINGS OF THE BEATITUDES IN THIS PASSAGE AS WELL?

WHY IS DYING TO SELF A DAILY TASK, NOT A ONE-TIME EVENT?

MEDITATION AND APPLICATION

READ MATTHEW 5:1-12 AGAIN SLOWLY AND REFLECT ON THE FOLLOWING QUESTIONS.

OF THE BEATITUDES THAT WE HAVE STUDIED IN THE PAST FOUR WEEKS, WHICH ONE STANDS OUT TO YOU MOST PERSONALLY?

HOW HAS YOUR MEMORIZATION OF THE BEATITUDES CHANGED THE WAY YOU THINK ABOUT JESUS AND THE CHRISTIAN LIFE?

WHAT DOES IT LOOK LIKE TO DIE TO YOURSELF TODAY? WHAT IS THE NARROW GATE BEFORE YOU?

EXERCISE

KYLE WRITES, "MOST OF US WOULD LIKE TO HAVE THE EXPERIENCE OF SERVING GOD IN SOME SIGNIFICANT WAY. WE PROBABLY EVEN HAVE SOME IDEAS ABOUT WHAT THAT WOULD BE. TRY COMPLETING THIS SENTENCE."

"MORE THAN ANYTHING, I WANT GOD TO USE ME TO

_____."

REFLECTION & REVIEW

Congratulations on reaching the end of *The End of Me* study Journal!

Today, review the Beatitudes and some of the major themes we've discussed over the past four weeks. What has been most meaningful to you? Where do you sense God inviting you to a new place of freedom and life in Christ?

Reflecting on the past four weeks, what do these statements mean to you? Put them into your own words.

You must be broken to be whole:

You must mourn to be happy:

You must be authentic to be accepted:

You must be empty to be filled:

SCRIPTURE MEMORY

REVIEW MATTHEW 5:1-12

NOW WHEN JESUS SAW THE CROWDS, HE WENT UP ON A MOUNTAINSIDE AND SAT DOWN. AND HE BEGAN TO TEACH THEM. HE SAID: BLESSED ARE THE POOR IN SPIRIT, FOR THEIRS IS THE KINGDOM OF HEAVEN. BLESSED ARE THOSE WHO MOURN, FOR THEY WILL BE COMFORTED. BLESSED ARE THE MEEK, FOR THEY WILL INHERIT THE EARTH. BLESSED ARE THOSE WHO HUNGER AND THIRST FOR RIGHTEOUSNESS, FOR THEY WILL BE FILLED. BLESSED ARE THE MERCIFUL, FOR THEY WILL BE SHOWN MERCY. BLESSED ARE THE PURE IN HEART, FOR THEY WILL SEE GOD. BLESSED ARE THE PEACEMAKERS, FOR THEY WILL BE CALLED CHILDREN OF GOD. BLESSED ARE THOSE WHO ARE PERSECUTED BECAUSE OF RIGHTEOUSNESS, FOR THEIRS IS THE KINGDOM OF HEAVEN. BLESSED ARE YOU WHEN PEOPLE INSULT YOU, PERSECUTE YOU AND FALSELY SAY ALL KINDS OF EVIL AGAINST YOU BECAUSE OF ME. REJOICE AND BE GLAD, BECAUSE GREAT IS YOUR REWARD IN HEAVEN, FOR IN THE SAME WAY THEY PERSECUTED THE PROPHETS WHO WERE BEFORE YOU.

QUESTIONS FOR REFLECTION

BASED ON YOUR WEEK'S READING AND REFLECTION, ANSWER THE FOLLOWING QUESTIONS.

WHAT WAS THE MOST SIGNIFICANT THING I LEARNED ABOUT JESUS AND THE CHRISTIAN LIFE OVER THE LAST 28 DAYS?

WHAT WAS THE MOST SIGNIFICANT THING I LEARNED ABOUT POVERTY OF SPIRIT, BROKENNESS, AND WHOLENESS THIS PAST MONTH?

WHAT WAS THE MOST SIGNIFICANT THING I LEARNED ABOUT MYSELF THIS PAST MONTH?

WHAT WOULD MY LIFE LOOK LIKE IF I FULLY BELIEVED AND LIVED EVERYTHING I READ AND WROTE THIS PAST MONTH?

REFERENCES

Idleman, Kyle. *The End of Me.* Colorado Springs, CO: David C Cook, 2015. Print.

Andrew Davis, "An Approach to Extended Memorization of Scripture." http://www.fbcdurham.org/wp-content/uploads/2015/07/Scripture-Memory-Booklet-for-Publication-Website-Layout.pdf

Jonathan Pennington, *The Sermon on the Mount and Human Flourishing: A Theological Commentary,* xv.

Andrew T. Jebb, et al. "Happiness, Income Satiation, and Turning Points around the World," *Nature Human Behavior* 2, 33-38 (2018).

Chuck DeGroat, *Wholeheartedness: Busyness, Exhaustion, and Healing the Divided Self,* 7.

Frederick Dale Bruner, *The Christbook: Matthew, A Commentary,* 162-168.

Oswald Chambers, *Biblical Theology,* 100, 107. Quoted in Elmer Towns, "The Meaning of Heart in the New Testament." https://biblicalstudies.org.uk/pdf/grace-journal/12-1_36.pdf

Mother Teresa if Calcutta, *Life in the Spirit: Reflections, Meditations, Prayers,* ed. Kathryn Spink (San Francisco: HarperCollins, 1983), 31.

D.L. Moody, quotes in Martin H. Manser, comp., *The Westminster Collection of Christian Quotations: Over 6,000 quotations arranged by Theme* (Louisville, KY: Westminster John Knox Press, 2001), 47.